An Award-Winning Teacher's Plan
to Prepare Your Child for School

Ready for
Kindergarten

S H A R O N   W I L K I N S

ILLUSTRATIONS BY MONA DALY

ZondervanPublishingHouse
Grand Rapids, Michigan
A Division of HarperCollinsPublishers

MOTHERS OF
MⓋPS.
PRESCHOOLERS

To Mom, my first teacher who believed in me and never let me
forget I was special. To my husband, Skip, and our two daughters,
Jenn and Melissa, who do all the things a writer needs—
love, encourage, edit, and most of all, believe in me.

Ready for Kindergarten
Copyright © 1996 by Sharon Anne Wilkins
First Zondervan edition 2000

Requests for information should be addressed to:
Zondervan Publishing House
Grand Rapids, Michigan 49530

Library of Congress Cataloging-in-Publication Data

Wilkins, Sharon Anne.
    Ready for kindergarten : an award winning teacher's plan to prepare your child for school /
  Sharon Wilkins.
        p.   cm.
    Originally published: Sisters, Or. : Gold'n'Honey Books, ©1996.
    ISBN: 0–310–23659–2 (softcover)
    1. Readiness for school. 2. Kindergarten. I. Title.
  LB1132.W55 2000

                                                       00–021528
                                                          CIP

Edited by Scharlotte Rich
Designed by David Carlson
Cover photo by Linda Bohm © 1996
Illustrations © 1996 by Mona Daly

Printed in the United States of America

00 01 02 03 04 05 /DC/ 10 9 8 7 6 5 4 3 2

Introduction

YOU are the most important teacher your child will ever have!

The activities in this book will help you provide your child with the foundation for a successful year in kindergarten. After completing this book, I hope you will walk away on the first day of kindergarten confident of your child's abilities to succeed, having taught your child new skills, a greater kindness toward others, and a new independence.

These 156 "kid-tested" activities are *fun, quick,* and developmentally appropriate for children ages four through six. Your child will be involved in a variety of learning areas including an appreciation for God, pre-reading skills, math, science, music, language, art, and activities to help your child get along with others. There is a small journal to jot down memorable moments.

Jesus said, "a little child shall lead them." Take your child's hand as together you enjoy *learning, laughter, and most of all, love.*

Week One: What's a Row?

A Minute for Mom: *For the mother is and must be, whether she knows it or not, the greatest, strongest, and most lasting teacher her children have.*—Hannah Whitall Smith

All in a Row!

Materials:
Five toys

Activity: It is important for your child to understand what a row is on a piece of paper. Start with concrete objects first.

Help your child collect five small toys. Ask him to put them in a row. Give help if needed.

Now put the five toys in a pile and see if he can make a row again by himself. Ask your child to touch the beginning of the row. Talk about the first, second, and third places. Compliment him for being a good listener!

A Minute for Mom: *It is more blessed to give than to receive.*—Acts 20:35

What's Missing?

Activity: Place five objects in a row on a table. Ask your child if the objects are in a circle or in a row. Next have her put them in a circle or a row. Do this several times until your child is confident using these terms.

Now let your child study them for a few seconds. Have your child turn away and not look while you take one object away. Have her look at the objects again to guess which object is missing. If it is too difficult for your child with five objects, try the game with two or three and gradually build up to five.

Always stop and have a snack or playtime when your child seems ready to change activities.

Materials:
Five different small objects (pencil, button, rock, spoon, etc.)

day 3

A Minute for Mom: *Dear God, too often my time is spent with work or dust cloths and cleaning fluids. Please help me to set good priorities so that I can share precious time with my child.*

I See It

Materials:
A piece of construction paper

Crayons or colored markers

Activity: Draw five small pictures in a row (a tree, balloon, apple, star, pizza). Talk about the pictures with your child. Ask her if the pictures are in a circle or a row. Ask which picture is first. Repeat the activity by asking your child to draw five small pictures in a row.

Talk about school. Tell your child that the teacher will talk about pictures in a row. Play the row game from Day 2.

Journal thoughts to remember…

A Minute for Mom: *Dear God, I know that for children, learning can be bumpy. Please shower me with patience.*

My First Letter

Activity: Mix flour and salt. Add a little water at a time, mixing as you pour to form a ball. Knead ten minutes until dough has a smooth, firm consistency. Enjoy conversation as you make the bread dough. If your child gets tired kneading, encourage him not to give up. Help your child make the first letter in his name. Make a hole at the top with a pencil before baking. Bake at 325° for thirty minutes until light brown. Do not eat!

Hang the letter on a wall or save it for your Christmas tree.

Materials:
2 c. flour

1 c. salt...
and patience!

1 c. water

Mixing bowl

day 2

A Minute for Mom: *Anyone who will not receive the kingdom of God like a little child will never enter it.*— Luke 18:17b

Shaving Mania

Materials:

Shaving cream

Old shirt

Activity: Put an old shirt on your child to wear for this "super fun" activity. Shaving cream is messy but easy to clean up. Warn your child not to touch his mouth or his eyes with the shaving cream.

Put a little shaving cream on your kitchen table and smooth it out so your child can touch, explore, and create. YOU try some, too. Be a part of your child's world!

After about five minutes of fun, ask your child if he remembers how to make the first letter in his name. If not, guide your child's finger, printing from top to bottom to form the letter together. Now encourage your child to practice making the letter. It's *easy* to erase mistakes with shaving cream and try again. (If the shaving cream starts to dry up, squirt more onto the table.)

A Minute for Mom: *Dear God, help me to remember how it feels to be a child. Please help me have joy and patience… especially when teaching my child new things!*

Printing in Sand or Salt

Activity: Fill a shoe box lid with approximately 1/2 inch of sand or salt. With your finger, print the first letter of your child's name in capital form in the sand or salt. Have your child copy the letter you made. Now let your child print a letter or shape and you copy it. *Praise* the child and have *fun!* Discuss curved and straight lines in the capital letter.

Now is a good time to explain that a letter can be printed two ways—capital and lowercase (e.g., "A, a"). Demonstrate capital and lowercase letters to your child by printing his first name on paper with a beginning capital letter and the rest of the letters lowercase.

Journal thoughts to remember…

Materials:

Empty shoe box lid

Sand or salt

Paper and Marker

A Minute for Mom: *Even when freshly washed and relieved of all obvious confections, children tend to be sticky.* —Fran Lebowitz

Just a Little Bit of Glue Will Do

Materials:

Old news-
paper

A pair of
child's safety
scissors

White liquid
glue

A piece of
paper,
approximately
eight and
a half by
eleven inches

Activity: Using any page of the newspaper, ask your child if she can find the first letter of her name and cut it out. Encourage your child to cut out any other letters or numbers that she knows. Watch to see that your child's thumb is on the top position of the scissors when cutting. *Praise* your child's efforts!

Using the tune of "Mary Had a Little Lamb," sing these words:

Just a little bit of glue,
bit of glue, bit of glue
Just a little bit of glue
Is all I have to do!

Let your child put "a little bit" of glue on the back of her cutouts and glue onto a piece of paper. Print "(<u>child's name</u>) is awesome!"

A Minute for Mom: *Dear God, help me to realize that I once needed a mother to show me a simple task, too.*

I'm Tops with Tape

Activity: Using an old toy catalogue, have your child cut out pictures of his favorite toys. (Make sure your child's thumb is in the top position of the scissors when cutting.)

Show your child how to tear off an ample piece of scotch tape to make a picture stick. Have him practice tearing a piece of tape and sticking each picture onto the paper, plate, or bag. Print "(<u>child's name</u>)'s favorite toys."

Thank your child for cleaning up and putting the materials away after the activity. Tell your child thanks for "sticking with it" until the mess is cleaned up. Smile and wink! Your child will really know you appreciate it.

Materials:
Old toy catalogue

A pair of child's safety scissors

A piece of paper, plastic plate, or paper bag

Tape

day 3

A Minute for Mom: *The mother's heart is the child's schoolroom.*—Henry Ward Beecher

Being Safe with Staplers

Materials:
Small bag

Magnifying glass (optional)

Stapler

Two pieces of paper, approximately eight and a half by eleven inches

Activity: Let your child look at a stapler. Ask her to tell you what she knows about a stapler. Mention that this tool should be used safely. Point out that it is shaped like an alligator's mouth and that she should *never* put her fingers inside where the paper gets stapled.

Now fold a piece of paper. Lay it in the proper place to be stapled. Let your child put her hands on top of the stapler and press down to staple the paper. Now, have her fold a piece of paper and staple it with your supervision. *Praise* your child for being such a good listener! Encourage your child to draw a picture on the inside of the little book she has made.

Journal thoughts to remember…

A Minute for Mom: *Dear God, help me rejoice in the beauties you have given me, and may I see them anew through my child's eyes.*

Nature Walk

Activity: Walk together and enjoy God's beautiful outdoors. Give your child a bag to collect things. As you open your front door, ask your child to discuss all the interesting things he sees (leaves, grass, a bug, etc.). Look closely at those things. A magnifier would be great! Save a small sample of interesting things in the bag.

Point out your house number. Ask your child if he knows any of the numbers.

Walk and observe the neighborhood beauty. Locate your street name sign. Discuss the letters. Review your house number and street name.

At home, print the house number and street name on the bag, display and discuss your child's treasures, and enjoy conversation about God's earth!

Materials:
Small bag

Magnifying glass (optional)

Week Four: My Street and God's Too

A Minute for Mom: *Dear God, when I think about the awesome responsibility of raising a child, help me to rest in your arms...to feel your assurance and peace knowing you will always be by my side.*

Play, Practice, Perform!

Materials:
Three-by-five-inch index cards or paper cut to this size

Crayons, pencils, or colored markers

Activity: Review your child's house number. Print each number on a separate card. Make two sets.

Give your child one set. Lay your cards on the table in random order. See if your child can put them in order.

Encourage your child even if the wrong number is chosen. Tell her, "It's great to see you trying...I'm proud of you," or "You almost got it right. Great!"

A Minute for Mom: *No man is poor who has had a godly mother.*
—Abraham Lincoln

day

3

I Know Where I Live

Activity: Review your child's address. Play a game. Give two choices when asking him to name your street ("Do you live on Elm Street in Gilbert or on Davis Street in Gilbert?"). This limits his choices and gives him one chance in two to get a correct answer! Now discuss the name of your town.

Using about five paper envelopes with the flap up for a roof, create your street together as a family. Decorate each envelope with doors, windows, house numbers, etc. A paper towel tube could become the street sign. Tell him that many streets make up your town.

Journal thoughts to remember…

Materials:
Approximately five paper envelopes

Crayons or colored markers

day

1

A Minute for Mom: *My mother was the source from which I derived the guiding principles of my life.*—John Wesley

Wow! God Is Creative

Materials:

Paper plate

Liquid glue
or scotch tape

Paper bag

Activity: Give your child a bag to collect a variety of leaves from trees while you walk around your yard or neighborhood. Discuss how boring the world would be if God had only given us one kind of leaf to enjoy. Talk about God's creativity!

Discuss similarities and differences in the leaves. For example, size, colors, patterns, and shapes. Leaves are environmentally important to us. They provide our oxygen so we can breathe. We need to take care of the trees God gave us.

Count the leaves. Sort them by size (small, medium, large) and count each group. Which size has more, less, the same? Glue the leaves onto a paper plate. (Praise your child for using "just a little bit" of glue). "Leave" your child's work on a wall to be enjoyed by the family.

Week Five: Leafy Ideas

A Minute for Mom: *Each of you should look not only to your own interests, but also to the interests of others. Your attitude should be the same as that of Christ Jesus.*—Philippians 2:4-5

Exploring

Activity: Call family members and friends and ask them to pick five different leaves from their yards and place them in bags. Once you receive the bags, give your child a different bag to collect five different leaves from plants in your yard or neighborhood. Lay your child's leaves on a table.

Materials:
A small bag

A family or friend's bag of leaves

Let your child pick one leaf at a time out of the other bags. Does it match any of your child's leaves? Discuss similarities and differences in the leaves. Continue until all the leaves have been examined.

Have fun sorting the leaves first by color (light and dark), size, shape, etc. Ask your child, "Why do you think God made so many different leaves? Do you have a favorite? Do you think bugs have favorite leaves, too?"

day 3

A Minute for Mom: *Kind words can be short and easy to speak, but their echoes are truly endless.*—Mother Teresa

A One-Minute Hug with Eyes

Materials:
One minute of uninter-rupted time

Bag of leaves

Activity: Play with the leaves from yesterday. Enjoy a conversation with your child and ask, "Does God want us to take care of his plants and trees? Why?" Be accepting of his thoughts. Don't talk *to* your child, talk *with him*.

Give your child a loving "hug with your eyes." For *one-minute*, continue to look at your child while he talks to you. Turn off the TV and if someone calls, let the phone ring! Enjoy his facial expressions. This one minute person-al gaze into his eyes will let your child feel loved. You are showing him that "looking at someone when he is talking" is an important part of respect!

Journal thoughts to remember...

A Minute for Mom: *I find life an exciting business, and most exciting when it is lived for others.*—Helen Keller

Fill It Up!

Activity: During bath time, let your child explore with a variety of plastic containers—empty milk gallons, half-gallons, quarts, etc. Measuring cups are great, too.

Watch her learn while playing. Ask questions such as: How many cups does it take to fill the half-gallon? The quart? Which one holds the least amount of water?

Your child will not only come out cleaner but *clearer* about volume and math terms.

Materials:
Empty plastic containers (milk gallon, half-gallon, quart, etc.)

day 2

A Minute for Mom: *Dear God, sometimes I am too busy even to smile at my child. Please remind me to practice simple kindness.*

Water Paint

Materials:

Two old
paint brushes

A bucket to
hold water

Activity: Find a couple of old paint brushes. Fill a bucket with water and join your child for fun and a simple lesson about evaporation!

Explore painting with water outside on the sidewalk. If you don't have a sidewalk, use the side of your house. Make designs, letters (practice making the first letter in her name), numbers (paint the address of your house), and write words such as "I love you."

When the water begins disappearing on the side-walk, ask your child where she thinks it went. Briefly explain how it evaporated into the air.

A Minute for Mom: *Dear God, open my eyes and help me see how to make you real to my child, even when we're only blowing bubbles.*

Bubble Blowout

Activity: Add one cup of liquid soap to your child's bath water. Talk about the safe practice of not breathing in through the straw when making bubbles.

Give your child a straw to create a bath of bubbles by blowing through the straw. Join in the fun!

Ask your child, "Are you glad God made water? Why? Water is used to clean us, but can you think of other ways we use water?" While tucking your child into bed, thank God for water.

Journal thoughts to remember…

Materials:
Approximately one cup liquid soap

Two straws

A Minute for Mom: *Is it possible that I am so busy doing that I no longer have time to enjoy being?*—Wilson

A Library Visit

Materials:
Time and
transportation!

Activity: Visit a library and check out books. Show your child how to sign up for a library card. Enjoy the book area for children. In addition to books, see if they have puzzles, listening centers, games, and other activities.

Find a cozy area, hold your child in your lap, and read a book. Try to make this moment a time you both will remember. Discuss the proper care of books, how to gently turn pages, and the importance of having clean hands.

Children want to be like their parents. Read to your child every day so she will see your love and appreciation of books. Books can make your child laugh, expand her world, and teach concepts.

A Minute for Mom: *Pleasant words are a honeycomb, sweet to the soul and healing to the bones.*—Proverbs 16:24

A Cozy Moment

Activity: Read a book to your child every day. Try to make time for a close, quiet moment when both of you can enjoy and delight in a book. After you read a book, explain what the word "character" means. Ask her who her favorite character was or what part of the story she liked the most.

Show her which part of the book is the cover, locate the page numbers, and have her guess where the first word on every page is. This is a beginning of learning that words go from left to right.

Research has shown that when parents frequently read to their children, they become better readers.

You can help your child become a successful reader!

Materials:
A good children's book

day 3

A Minute for Mom: *Be assured, if you walk with Him and look to Him and expect help from Him, He will never fail you.*
—George Mueller

Books and Problems

Materials:
A good book

Activity: If you have issues to discuss with your child such as biting, yelling, being a bully, lying, anger, divorce, or a new baby, ask a librarian for a good children's book to read to your child that would help with the situation. Books are a wonderful way to open up issues for discussion. They can help you and your child share personal feelings and together, discuss ideas for improvement.

You might even share a time when you felt the same way as your child. For example, even Jesus got angry, but it was righteous anger, handled well.

Journal thoughts to remember…

A Minute for Mom: *Love is patient.*—1 Corinthians 13:4a

Cooking Up a Treat

Activity: Cooking is a great learning experience for your child. Using the ingredients listed, you and your child can make a peanut butter playdough recipe. It might be messy, but have patience. Children learn best when they are actively involved.

Let your child measure and mix the peanut butter and honey. Slowly add the powdered milk until a workable consistency is achieved.

Encourage your child to make something. Then see if he can make what you make—a number, letter, shape, etc. *Eat up!*

Materials:

1 c. peanut butter

1 tbls. honey

1 c. powdered milk

Spoon and bowl

Week Eight: Measuring Up

A Minute for Mom: *Children have never been very good at listening to their elders, but they have never failed to imitate them.* —James Baldwin

Stringing You Along

Materials:

A piece of string approximately eight inches long

A twelve-inch ruler

Household objects (spoon)

Activity: Using the piece of string and an object in your home such as a spoon, show your child how to lay the string straight and measure an object from one end to the other. Is the spoon shorter or longer than the string?

Show him the twelve-inch ruler. Ask your child to describe what he sees. Can he find the number six? Mention that it is in the middle. Have your child observe how the numbers get bigger, starting with number one.

Challenge your child to find something in the house that is twelve inches long or use a meter stick, whichever is handy.

A Minute for Mom: *Dear God, I want to measure up as a mom. Continue to mold me so my child will someday say, "I always felt so loved, and to think, God loves me even more!"*

Making a Measuring Tool

Activity: Help your child make a unit of measurement. Make a small one first by laying five to eight dry beans in a line in the middle of the sticky side of transparent packing tape. (Other objects could also be used, such as plastic milk bottle caps.) Fold the tape over and secure the beans inside.

Show your child a utensil and ask if she thinks the "bean tape" will be longer or shorter than the utensil you are showing. Watch your child measure. Make sure she starts at one end and lays the measuring tool straight. *Measure other things, too!*

Journal thoughts to remember…

Materials:
A small piece of transparent packing tape

Objects such as dry beans or milk bottle caps

Week Nine: I'm Never Alone

A Minute for Mom: *Never will I leave you.*—Hebrews 13:5b

God Gives Courage

Materials:
A Bible

Activity: Talk about occasions when your child showed courage. For example, the time he kept trying to ride his bike while a little scared. Or perhaps your child was afraid of the dark but quietly went to sleep. Tell your child you are thankful he has courage.

Hold your child on your lap and mention five very important words in the Bible—"Never will I leave you." Mention that Jesus told his friends those words. He wanted them to have courage and to know that he would always be there for them. Tell your child that going to kindergarten on the first day will take courage because it will be new, but not to be afraid because he will not be alone. Jesus will be with him.

Have your child hold up a hand and point to each finger as you repeat the verse "Never will I leave you."

A Minute for Mom: *Dear God, help me to have the right words when I talk to my child about you.*

Mom's Feelings

Activity: When you tuck your child into bed tonight, ask her to hold up a hand and say the five important words in the Bible that you talked about earlier.

Materials:
Extra time tucking your child into bed

As you sit together, ask your child what it means to never leave someone. Then tell her a time when you were lonely or were afraid to try something new, like when you went to a new school. Talk about your feelings and how you overcame them. Did you find enough courage? Did you pray?

Tell your child to always remember she is never alone!

day 3

Week Nine: I'm Never Alone

A Minute for Mom: *Dear God, sometimes it's hard to realize children have feelings just as adults do. Help me to remember daily that my child's world is never less important than my world!*

Believing

Materials:
Time together

Activity: Talk about the story of Noah's ark and how God's heart was filled with pain because the people did not worship him. Tell your child that God told Noah how to build the ark to save Noah's family because they loved God. Talk about Noah's courage.

Have your child count the five words "Never will I leave you" on her fingers. Make a promise that if either of you is scared, you'll remind each other of the five words.

Journal thoughts to remember…

A Minute for Mom: *Surprises are a wonderful way to say I love you.*

Surprise! Your Choice!

Activity: Surprise your child! Turn off a TV program you are watching. Tell your child she is much more important than television and that you want to do something with her.

Ask your child what game or activity she would like to do. (For example, have a pillow fight, use old socks and make puppets, read a book, etc.)

After your together-time, give your child a big hug and say three wonderful words... I LOVE YOU!

Materials: A game or activity of your child's choice

Week Ten: Showing Respect

A Minute for Mom: *Children need models more than they need critics.*—Joseph Joubert

Oops!
My Crayons Fell

Materials:
Together-time

Box of
crayons

Activity: Play pretend with your child. Hold a box of crayons in your hand and "accidentally" drop them.

Ask your child what he would do if that happened to another child in the classroom at school. Let your child share ideas. Ask your child how a person would feel if other children laughed when the crayons were dropped. Mention that he will have choices to make at school because things like this happen.

Ask your child what he thinks it means to respect somebody. Ask if God wants us to respect each other. Thank your child for listening to you right now because he is showing respect.

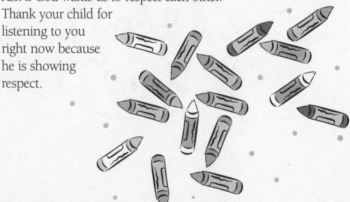

A Minute for Mom: *A mother is not a person to lean on but a person to make leaning unnecessary.*—Dorothy Canfield Fisher

See the Good

Activity: Watch to see your child doing something good, like sharing with a friend, putting toys away, taking her dishes to the sink, etc. Thank your child for being kind. Mention that acting that way is showing respect for the other person.

Ask your child for ideas for showing respect in kindergarten, such as putting the classroom toys away, making sure all her papers get home, and bringing home her coat or sweater every day. Tell her that trying to do these things shows kindness and respect.

Discuss how Jesus showed kindness and respect to people.

Journal thoughts to remember…

Materials:
A watchful eye

A Minute for Mom: *Dear God, help me to give my worries of today to you, so that I may give myself to my child.*

Playdough Shapes

Materials:

1 c. flour

2 tsp. cream of tartar

1 tbls. vegetable oil

1 c. water

1/2 c. salt

Few drops of food coloring

Spoon

Mixing bowl

Activity: Make this easy playdough recipe. Mix ingredients together in a pan. Cook three minutes on medium heat. Stir constantly. Dough will stick to the spoon. Cool and knead about ten minutes. Store in a covered container or plastic bag. This is not edible.

Join in the fun! With your child, make animals, numbers, letters, etc. Now play the Copy Cat Game. You make a shape and your child tries to make one, too. Start with a circle, then try a triangle, square, and rectangle. Ask him what is alike and different when comparing two shapes. *Smile* often and experience the "joy" of conversation.

Eating Shapes

Activity: Take a long graham cracker. Ask your child what shape it is. Break it in half and talk about the square shapes. Then take one square and break it in half to make two rectangles. You can even teach addition by showing that one square plus one square equals a rectangle! Let your child eat each shape after telling you the name of the shape.

Children love to be teachers! It's your turn to be the student. Let your child give you a graham cracker and you name the different shapes.

Materials:
Graham crackers

Week Eleven: Fun with Shapes

A Minute for Mom: *Dear God, I want to have more "fun" being a mom. Please take away my worries and problems of this moment and replace them with love and laughter.*

Finger Painting with Pudding

Materials:
A package of pudding

Activity: Make your child's favorite pudding. Then have her wash her hands while you wash the kitchen table.

Let your child finger paint with pudding! After about five minutes of fun, ask your child to make the first letter in her name and the basic shapes. *Encourage* her efforts. Being five means your child can go to kindergarten, so you could compliment your child on how she is growing and show her how to make the number five in the pudding.

This should be a fun experience so provide plenty of time for your child to explore while finger painting. Clean up is easy! YUM!!!

Journal thoughts to remember…

A Minute for Mom: *Being a mother is one of the highest-salaried jobs in my field since the payment is pure love.*
—Mildred Vermont

Colors in the Grocery Store

Activity: When you take your child to the grocery store, spend time in the fruit and vegetable aisle looking at all the beautiful colors of food God has provided for us.

Materials:
Trip to the grocery store

If she is enjoying the time, capture this moment and teach some names of fruits and vegetables. Challenge your child to find colors in the fruits and vegetables. Play "I Spy" something—red, green, blue, etc.. See if your child can find what you are spying. Share the names of some of the strange foods. Try eating a different fruit or vegetable every few weeks. (Coconuts are especially fun!)

Point out the scale for weighing food. Let your child pick out some food to weigh and guess how many pounds it will be. You might want to do this on a day when you aren't in a hurry and don't have a lot of groceries to buy! Or make it a separate "field trip."

day 2

A Minute for Mom: *Dear God, I desire more spontaneity! Please restore it in me.*

Cheer for Colors

Materials:
Energy to cheer

Two red apples

Activity: Sometime when you're eating red apples, surprise your child and say that you know how to do a cheer to spell the word "red." Bend down and when you touch the ground say the letter "R." Then stand up, put your hands on your hips, and say "E." Now stretch your arms up high and say "D." Then jump up with your hands stretched high and yell "RED." Encourage your child to do the cheer a couple of times and enjoy some laughter together.

Sing to the tune of "Mary Had a Little Lamb":

I can spell the color red,
color red, color red,
I can spell the color red,
It's simple—R-E-D.

A Minute for Mom: *Cleaning your house while your kids are still growing is like shoveling the walk before it stops snowing.* —Phyllis Diller

Sorting by Color

Activity: Place approximately 1/4 cup of cereal on a table. Help your child sort the pieces in rows by color. Count and record the total for each row on a small piece of paper. You or your child can put the total number at the end of each row.

    Which row is the longest? Shortest? Most? Least? Equal? When finished, let your child eat the "fruits" of this sorting activity! *Praise* his efforts!

Journal thoughts to remember…

Materials:
A handful of colored cereal

day

1

A Minute for Mom: *You may occasionally give out—but never give up.*—Mary Crowley

I Think I Can!

Materials:
Book:
*The Little
Engine That
Could*

Activity: Read or tell the classic story, *The Little Engine That Could.*

Ask your child to tell you about his favorite part of the story. Ask him what the little engine did that was so kind.

Discuss how the little engine didn't know if he could get the whole train over the mountain, but he had a good attitude and was willing to try.

Ask your child what he would do if the kindergarten teacher asked him to print the number 5 and your child didn't know how. (Be accepting of his ideas, such as asking a friend, asking the teacher, practicing, etc.)

Hug your child and compliment him on his ideas. Say, "I'm glad you have a good attitude and keep trying when you have hard things to do."

A Minute for Mom: *Dear God, please help me to find the child in myself again.*

I Know I Can!

Activity: Visit the grocery store and ask for a variety of boxes. They make wonderful, creative toys for children and they're free, so fill your car!

Put the boxes in your backyard and ask your child to make a train. Tell her, "I think you can!" Let your child create, explore, and make a train using markers, crayons, yarn, tempera paint, etc. You could cut holes out of the box for the engine so your child could be the engineer. Now crawl in.

Invite a friend over. Stand back and enjoy watching your creative genius at work!

When you tuck your child into bed, talk about how creative she was in building the train and tell her, "I knew you could do it!"

Materials:
Free cardboard boxes from a grocery store

Crayons, colored markers

Scraps of other materials (fabric, paper tubes, etc.)

day 3

A Minute for Mom: *Dear God, life isn't easy a lot of the time. Please help me to instill the importance of "really trying" in my child so he develops a strong spirit about life.*

Message in a Song

Materials:
None

Activity: Sing the song, "Itsy Bitsy Spider." Ask your child whether or not the spider gave up when the rain came down.

Tell your child God wants us to try, too. Ask your child, "If you can't write the letter 'b' [or something else the child is working on] right away, what do you think you should do?" (Be accepting of his ideas, such as getting someone to help him or practicing.)

Thank your child for realizing it's important to try.

Journal thoughts to remember…

A Minute for Mom: *One person can make a difference and every person should try.*—John F. Kennedy

Following Directions

Activity: Using playdough, give specific directions of things to make. *Remember, smile often!* It's an important way to show your love.

Materials:
Playdough from Week 11, Day 1

Ask your child to make:

1. a flat circle
2. a flat square

Have your child place the circular shape on top of the square shape. Discuss what the two shapes together could be. Now you be the student. Let your child give you directions of things to make with playdough.

Praise your child for her good listening and mention how much the teacher will appreciate good listeners in the classroom. Discuss briefly how it feels when someone doesn't listen, that we feel left out. Tell your child you like it when she listens to you.

day 2

A Minute for Mom: *By perseverance the snail reached the ark.*
—Charles Spurgeon

I Can Listen!

Materials:
A kitchen chair

Activity: Place one kitchen chair in the center of a room. Give your child directions:

1. Walk around the chair slowly.
2. Stand beside the chair.
3. Sit on the chair quietly.
4. Put your elbow on the chair.

If he doesn't understand at times, be gentle, *smile,* and repeat the direction. Take turns and let your child give you directions.

Sing this song to the tune of "Are You Sleeping?":

I can listen,
I can listen,
Watch me try,
Watch me try,
Stop now and be quiet,
So can I!
So can I!

A Minute for Mom: *God pardons like a mother who kisses away the repentant tears of her child.*—Henry Ward Beecher

Solving Problems Takes Listening

Activity: Try to catch your child *not* getting along with her friend. Kneel by them and separate the two. Tell the children each will have a chance to share what happened, but that when one is talking, the other person must be quiet and listen. After each child shares her side of the story, tell them that God gave each a good mind and that you know the two of them can solve the problem.

Materials:
None

Leave and do other things, but stay nearby in case you are needed. Hopefully, the children will be able to listen to each other and solve their problem. If not, help them come up with a solution. Ask the children how they felt when the other person listened.

Journal thoughts to remember…

Week Fifteen: Growing in Responsibility

A Minute for Mom: *Act as if what you do makes a difference. It does!*—William James

Setting the Table

Materials:

Silverware

Napkins

Activity: Let your child help set the table. Show him there is a place for everything—fork on the left on top of a napkin, the knife and spoon on the right. Each has its special place, just as his toys have a special place.

Mention that his kindergarten classroom will have special places for crayons, toys, books, and coats. Discuss what the classroom would look like if the children didn't put things in the right place. Talk about how hard it is to find things if they have no "home."

Ask your child if he has any ideas on how to keep the house picked up or where certain things should have a "home." Remember to thank him for being a helper when you see him carrying out some of his ideas.

This conversation could lead to a cleaner tomorrow—and growth in being more responsible!

A Minute for Mom: *Dear God, please help me to take the time to teach my child how to do things by herself. Sometimes it's easier for me to put the toys away, but I know I must teach my child to be responsible.*

I'm Capable!

Activity: With your child, make a list of activities she could do by herself. For example, making her bed, tearing lettuce for a salad, putting her toys away before getting out other toys or games, and taking her own dishes to the sink after meals.

Make a sign, printing your child's name and then the words "is responsible!" Your child could decorate it with colored markers.

Compliment your child on how responsible she can be.

Ask your child if she thinks Jesus was responsible. Why? Explain that when you are responsible, it means you can do things all by yourself, without being told.

Ask her if she can think of anything Jesus as a boy was capable of doing around a carpenter's shop.

Materials:
A piece of paper

Pencil, crayons, or colored markers

Week Fifteen: Growing in Responsibility

A Minute for Mom: *Motherhood is a mighty force that can help change the world!*—Sharon Wilkins

Family Discussion

Materials:
None

Activity: As a family, discuss how you are all part of a team and that each person has his own responsibilities. Each person should talk about several of his responsibilities.

Discuss some of Noah's jobs. Take turns naming other people in the Bible and some of their responsibilities.

When you tuck your child into bed, ask him what he thinks his responsibilities will be in kindergarten. Conclude by telling your child that his job will be to learn, meet new friends, and have fun!

Journal thoughts to remember...

A Minute for Mom: *What feeling is so nice as a child's hand in yours? So small, so soft and warm, like a kitten huddling in the shelter of your clasp.*—Marjorie Holmes

Movin' and Groovin'

Activity: Make a maraca out of small, empty tin cans. Check to make sure there are no rough edges around the open end. Let your child fill the cans with tiny items such as rocks, unpopped popcorn, or buttons, and tape paper over the open end. Play some music, and have your child create a rhythm.

Play the game Follow the Leader. As you make a motion with your body, have your child imitate you. Then change the motion for awhile and return to the original motion. Tell your child this is called a pattern—an AB pattern because you did two different motions.

Now let your child lead you in a body motion. When your child starts a second motion, compliment her for creating an AB pattern, too!

Materials:
Small empty tin cans

Small objects (buttons, popcorn, etc.)

Music

day **2**

A Minute for Mom: *All that I am or hope to be I owe to my angel mother. I remember my mother's prayers and they have always followed me. They have clung to me all my life.*
—Abraham Lincoln

Playing for God on My Guitar

Materials:

Empty
shoe box

Rubber bands

Other small
boxes
(optional)

Activity: Together create an instrument for your child to play while singing "Jesus Loves Me" and other favorite songs.

Simply stretch rubber bands over different areas of an open shoe box. Pluck the strings while you sing! Pretend it is a real guitar.

Try different shaped boxes and rubber bands to create a variety of sounds.

It's Kazoo Time

Activity: With your child, try making a kazoo! Let her decorate a small paper tube with crayons, markers, etc. Then cover one end of the paper tube tightly with wax paper. (Anchor with tight rubber band.) Finish by cutting about a quarter-inch hole near the wax paper end.

God created us with voices, so hum away!

Journal thoughts to remember...

Materials:

A small paper tube

Crayons, colored markers

A small piece of wax paper

A rubber band

A Minute for Mom: *The best minute you spend is the one you invest in people.*—Blanchard and Johnson

My Hands Are Special

Materials:
A small (twelve ounce) empty coffee can

A large old sock

Small household items

Activity: Tell your child that Jesus healed many people by touching them. Ask your child to show you his kind hands.

Now together create an instant "feely" game by placing a small empty coffee can with no rough edges into a large sock. Every family member should put two small objects into the can without telling anyone what they are. Then everyone should take a turn reaching into the can, feeling an item, and trying to identify the item while it's still inside the can.

During prayers at bedtime, thank God for making our hands.

A Minute for Mom: *If you're too busy to help those around you succeed, you're too busy.*—Bob Moawad

"Eye" Say, Thanks to God!

Activity: Cut paper squares approximately two by two inches and print your child's first name by writing one letter on each square. Help her print a star on three more squares.

Now section off two-by-two-inch squares on a rectangular strip of paper. Print your child's name with only one letter in each square. Lay this paper on a table so your child can see it.

Let your child pull one letter at a time out of the coffee can and try to match it on the rectangle strip. See if she can do this before getting three stars.

Help your child match the letters on the paper strip. Lavish her with praise for her effort.

Materials:
The coffee can and old sock from Week 17, Day 1

Two-by-two-inch plain squares of paper

A long rectangular strip of paper

day 3

A Minute for Mom: *I praise you because I am fearfully and wonderfully made.*—Psalm 139:14a

I Can Hear!

Materials:

A tape recorder

A blank tape

Activity: Review with your child how wonderfully we are made. Ask him what parts of the body were needed to play the coffee can games (Week 17, Days 1 and 2).

Using a tape recorder and a blank tape, let your child choose different sounds to record, such as dogs barking and someone brushing his teeth. Play the tape for the family after dinner to see if anyone can guess the sounds.

THANK GOD WE CAN HEAR!

Journal thoughts to remember...

A Minute for Mom: *There is no exercise better for the heart than reaching down and lifting people up.*—John A. Holmes

I Know How and When to Dial 9-1-1

Activity: Growing in confidence is important, and teaching your child how to become independent will build her self-esteem.

Tell your child she is old enough now to learn how to dial 9-1-1 in case of an emergency. Remind her of the importance of the telephone, that it is not a toy, and that 9-1-1 should never be dialed unless there is a real emergency. Discuss some examples.

Write the numbers on the paper in large lettering. Take time to teach your child where 9-1-1 is on the phone. Let your child practice saying, "I need help" slowly and clearly. (Note: Some phones have a special button just for 9-1-1.)

Give your child a *big* hug and thank her for being responsible.

Practice this activity once a week until you are sure your child can do it well. Be careful not to frighten your child. Emphasize that she is just learning a skill and will probably never have to use it.

Materials:
A telephone

Paper and marker or crayon

day 2

A Minute for Mom: *It's a fine thing to have ability, but the ability to discover ability in others is the true test.*—Elbert Hubbard

I Can Put My Toys Away

Materials:

Your child's toys

Clear plastic containers to organize toys

Activity: Training your child to clean up will help him become more responsible and independent.

Buy some clear plastic containers to store your child's toys in. Tell him you have a new rule that will help keep the house cleaner and safer. Ask your child what he thinks would happen if everyone left things scattered on the floor—someone could trip and fall, it would be hard to find certain things, etc. Together put your child's toys in clear containers in his bedroom.

Play with one of your child's favorite toys for a few minutes. When finished, ask what should be done with the toys. *Thank your child for being responsible and independent.*

A Minute for Mom: *Dear God, sometimes it is so much easier to do things for my child rather than teach my child to do them. Help me to change this about my life.*

Look What I Can Do!

Activity: Teaching your child to zip clothing, button a shirt, and tie shoes helps her become more independent and ready for school. Pick one skill your child needs help with and break it down into small steps. Learning to tie shoes, for example, can be a long process, so be patient and teach this independent skill one step at a time.

We feel good about ourselves when we can do things without help and your child does, too.

Compliment your child for trying! Diligence is a great quality to have in life!

Journal thoughts to remember…

Materials:
A shirt or blouse to button

A piece of clothing that has a zipper

Shoes with shoelaces

Week Nineteen: God's World

A Minute for Mom: *You carved no shapeless marble to some high-souled design, but with a finer sculpture, you shaped this soul of mine.*—Thomas Fessenden

Drop It!

Materials:
Water

A piece of wax paper, approximately eight by ten inches

A paper towel

Optional:
An eye-dropper

Activity: Let your child observe water drops on a piece of wax paper.

Have your child put drops of water on a piece of wax paper. (You might have to show your child how to use an eyedropper.)

Can your child make the water drops move by blowing gently? Can he drag a drop of water by pulling the eyedropper through it? Use a corner of a paper towel to soak up one drop at a time. Let your child be a scientist and investigate by trying different things. And it's easy to clean up! Give your child lots of opportunities to expand his curiosity and creativity. Sometimes just "messing around" is a great learning experience.

During prayers, thank God not only for water, but for our great minds!

A Minute for Mom: *The greatest difference which I find between my mother and the rest of the people is she felt a strong interest in the whole world and everything and everybody in it.*
—Mark Twain

Paint My Feet Like a Butterfly, Mom

Activity: Read Eric Carle's book, *The Hungry Caterpillar,* or perhaps other books about butterflies. Discuss their beauty with your child and how nice it was for God to give them to us to enjoy. Point out that butterflies are symmetrical (their colorful markings are the same on each of their wings).

Here comes the *fun* part. Outside, have your child sit in a chair while you paint the bottom of each bare foot the identical way; for example, both big toes yellow, other toes red, and the rest of the foot blue. Have your child step down on paper and then into a tub of water to wash off the paint. Draw wings on the paper that include her painted feet. Draw antennae, and now you have one of God's beautiful creations! On another day, try painting hands instead of feet.

Materials:
A plain piece of paper, approximately thirteen by twelve inches

Tempera paint (at least two colors)

day 3

Week Nineteen: God's World

A Minute for Mom: *Sons are a heritage from the LORD, children a reward from him.*—Psalm 127:3

I'm a Scientist!

Materials:

An apple core

A magnifying glass (optional)

Activity: Ask your child if she knows what an insect is. Tell her that God gave us many different kinds in the world and that an insect has six legs and three body parts.

Ask if your child knows what a scientist does. Discuss how a scientist looks at things and investigates them. Tell your child she can be a scientist, too. Let her put an apple core in the back yard and observe it daily, being careful she wears shoes and doesn't get too close to the ants or some other insects. (Some children are very allergic to insect bites.)

Journal thoughts to remember…

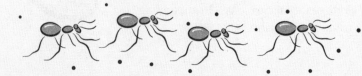

A Minute for Mom: *Dear God, help me to stop everything I'm doing when my child pretends to be reading to me.*

day
1

I Can Read!

Activity: Your child can become an author and illustrator of his own book!

Using magazines, food box labels, and newspapers, have your child help you cut out well-known words.

Glue each word onto a separate page. Staple the pages together on the left side. *Surprise!* Your child can read some of the words.

Enjoy listening to your child's comments as you do this activity together. Share loving words. Talking *with* your child and not *at* your child helps to build his self-esteem. Listen as your child "reads" to you.

Materials:
Plain paper, approximately six by eight inches

Child-safe scissors

White glue

Old magazines, food boxes, newspapers

Week Twenty: Books in the Making

A Minute for Mom: *When Mother Teresa received her Nobel Prize, she was asked, "What can we do to promote world peace?" She replied, "Go home and love your family."*—Anonymous

I'm an Author

Materials:

Ten plain sheets of paper, approximately four by six inches

A hole punch

Pencils, crayons, or colored markers

Activity: Show your child how to punch a hole in paper. Tell her it's time to make a number book using the hole punch.

Let your child punch one hole in one sheet of paper, two in another sheet, three in another, continuing until there are ten pages with hole punches. (If your child gets tired of punching, help her, or just make a book with five pages.) Staple the pages together to make a number book. Help your child print the numbers on each page. You could even print the number words so your child could "*read*" the number after counting the holes!

Print a title and let your child print her name as the author!

A Minute for Mom: *The nicest thing we can do for our heavenly Father is to be kind to one of his children.*—St. Teresa Avila

A Fascinating Object Book

Activity: Tell your child he is going to make a book using ten zip-lock sandwich bags.

Ask your child to put one small, interesting thing in each bag and seal it (e.g., penny, button, pebble). Print the name of the object on each bag using a permanent marker. Hole punch the same corner of each bag and bind with a piece of yarn.

Let your child read the book to others. Print a title and the word "by." Next have your child print his name and celebrate being an author!

Journal thoughts to remember…

Materials:

Ten zip-lock sandwich bags

A permanent marker

A hole punch

Small piece of yarn to bind book

day **1**

A Minute for Mom: *Let your light shine before men, that they may see your good deeds and praise your Father in heaven.* —Matthew 5:16

Flashlight Fun

Materials:

A flashlight

A light-colored piece of paper, approximately eight by eighteen inches

A dark-colored marker

Activity: Print the letters of your child's first name (each letter about four inches high) on a plain piece of paper using a dark-colored marker. Attach it to a wall in your child's bedroom so it can be seen when she is lying in bed.

When tucking your child into bed, turn off the bedroom lights and give your child a flashlight. Play a game and ask her to flash the light on the first letter in her name, then on the last letter, then on another letter. The next time, put the numbers one through ten or shapes of different colors on the door. Be sure to tell your child how smart she is!

Enjoy this peaceful moment with your child. Sing, "This Little Light of Mine" and describe to her how you saw her shining a light when she was kind to a particular person.

A Minute for Mom: *Dear God, when I grow old,
I don't want to wish I had spent more time with my child. Help
me to be able to say I took advantage of enjoying his presence.*

What's the Clue?

Activity: Tonight, play the "Clue" game before you say prayers
with your child. Give your child three clues about an object in
his bedroom and see if your child can guess which object you
are referring to. (In the beginning of the game, give easy clues,
and then gradually make it a little harder.) Describe only five
objects or fewer if you see your child losing interest.

Take turns and try to guess from your child's clues.

Materials:
None

day 3

A Minute for Mom: *If you have knowledge, let others light their candles at it.*—Margaret Fuller

A Cozy Light

Materials:
A candle and matches

Activity: At bedtime, snuggle cozily on the bed with your child. Talk about "a long time ago" when people had to use candles instead of electric lights. Light and hold a candle. (Tell your child to *never* play with matches.) Turn off all the other lights and enjoy the solitude of the moment.

Discuss how God wants each of us to be a light in the world. Ask your child what she thinks that means. Be accepting of all her ideas. If she responds with a far-out answer, say "that's interesting," showing respect for her thoughts.

Journal thoughts to remember...

A Minute for Mom: *A friend loves at all times.*—Proverbs 17:17

I'm a Friend

Activity: Without your child knowing, place a mirror inside a box with a lid. Hold your child on your lap and begin to tell him that soon he will see a very special person inside the box. First say, "I want to talk about what the word 'friend' means." You might ask:

Materials:
A box
with a lid

A mirror

1.Who are some of your friends?
2.What do your friends do that you like?
3.What could you do if you and your friend didn't get along?

Tell your child that God said a friend should love at all times and that the one your child will soon see inside the box is someone you love all the time.

Now take the lid off the box for your child to see their own reflection. *Surprise! It's you!*

Week Twenty-Two: Making Friends

A Minute for Mom: *A happy heart makes the face cheerful.*
—Proverbs 15:13

Friends

Materials:
Time

Patience

Activity: Invite a friend of your child's over to play. Before he comes, help your child plan some fun things to do with his friend. Plan a snack together for after playtime. Talk about sharing and being a good friend.

A Minute for Mom: *The fragrance always remains in the hand that gives the rose.*—Heda Bejar

A Friendship Tree

Activity: Invite three of your child's friends over for a friendship party. Tell them they were invited over because all of the children are good friends. At the kitchen table, show the children the branches in the containers. Explain that they are "friendship trees," and that the children are going to decorate their names to hang on the trees.

Help each child print his name on three pieces of paper using markers, scraps of fabric and paper, crayons, buttons, and glitter. Hang each name on the friends' trees and print on the container "_____'s friends!"

You could serve a snack, then let the children take home their trees.

Journal thoughts to remember…

Materials:
Four small branches anchored in containers (e.g., sand in four coffee cans)

Construction paper

Child-safe scissors

Crayons or colored markers

Assorted items such as fabric scraps, glitter, buttons, etc.

Week Twenty-Three: Scoop and Sort

A Minute for Mom: *Dear God, help me to make our home a place where my child's spirit can take wings. Please give me the wisdom, love, and patience I need to do this.*

Math Is Fun

Materials:
Different colored one-gallon milk tops (twenty or more)

Activity: Have your child grab two handfuls of colored milk tops. Encourage her to sort the tops by color in a line.

Help your child count each row of colors with her finger so that she doesn't say two numbers when counting one milk top. Print the total number at the end of each row.

Ask your child which color totaled the most, and which the least. Ask if any colors were the same (or equal).

Praise and smile! The effect is better than medicine.

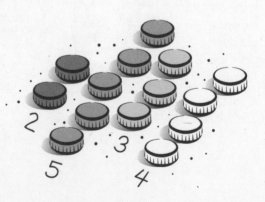

A Minute for Mom: *When losing his mother at the age of six, he said in later years, "I have carried the remembrance of her gentle voice and soothing touch all through my life."*—Ida Comstock Below

Check Out These Shoes!

Activity: Ask your child to "scoop" up about ten shoes in the house, taking only one shoe from a pair. Lay the shoes on the floor. (You will have no pairs.)

Together describe each shoe. Talk about the colors and the similarities and differences. Now have your child sort the shoes by big and little, and then count each group. Which group has more or less?

Next have your child sort by color, by new and old, and by those that have shoelaces versus those that do not. Ask your child to sort the shoes into other groups while you try to guess his criteria for sorting.

If your child has trouble with this concept, be patient. Play the game again tomorrow with ten different shoes, buttons or other objects around the house.

Materials:
8-10 single shoes

10 buttons (optional)

Week Twenty-Three: Scoop and Sort

A Minute for Mom: *Mothering does have its many pleasurable moments, but those come only with a total commitment of the will to weather all the sticky times in between.*—Stephen and Janet Bly

It's in the Bag!

Materials:
One small
bag of colored
candies (about
1.6 ounces)

Activity: Buy a small, individual bag of colored candies. Ask your child to sort the candy by color, then count and total each color. Make sure your child counts slowly, one by one.

Ask your child which color there was the most of in the package. Of which was there the least? As a challenge, ask how many more were in the greatest number than in another color.

Journal thoughts to remember…

A Minute for Mom: *It is possible to give without loving, but it is impossible to love without giving.*—R. Braunstein

I Can Fold It!

Activity: Fold a piece of paper in half. Explain which is the folded side (crease) and which is the open side.

Draw a half-circle on the fold and let your child cut it out to discover a whole circle! Fold another piece of paper and draw half of a heart. Help your child cut it out. *Surprise!* Give your child a big hug and print "I love you" inside the heart.

During this activity, it's important to review the terms *open* and *folded* sides. *Half* may also be a new vocabulary word.

To explain this further, fill a glass half full of water, or divide a cookie in half to share.

Materials:
Two pieces of paper, approximately eight by ten inches

Crayons

Child-safe scissors

day

2

A Minute for Mom: *Home sweet home—where each lives for the other, and all live for God.*—T. J. Bach

Who Is Second in Line?

Materials:
None

Activity: Ask your family or friends to make one line at the door. Ask your child, who is the tallest? Shortest? Who is first? Second? Third? Give your child *time to think* before offering any answers.

Expand the activity. Who was second to the breakfast table? Who was second to wake up this morning?

Explain that in school, the teacher will have the children line up when they leave the room to go to the playground, and to do other activities.

A Minute for Mom:
> There are teachings in earth and sky and air,
> The heavens the glory of God declare;
> But louder than voice, beneath, above,
> He is heard to speak in a mother's love. —Emily Taylor

Left? Is that Right?

Activity: Introduce the concept of "left" and "right." Tape a piece of string or yarn under your child's chin so it hangs down the middle of his body to divide it in half. Explain that everything on one side is "left." The other side is "right."

Standing behind your child so you can help him, ask him to wiggle the fingers on his left hand, wave his right hand, tap his left foot, and so forth. This is a difficult concept that should be integrated into your child's daily life. "Let's put on your *left* mitten." "Wave your *right* hand at Grandma."

Journal thoughts to remember…

Materials:
A piece of string or yarn, approximately three feet long

An abundance of patience …keep *smiling!*

day
1

Week Twenty-Five: Parts of the Puzzle

A Minute for Mom: *My mother was an angel on earth. She was a minister of blessing to all human beings within her sphere of action.* —John Quincy Adams

It Puzzles Me!

Materials:
A child's puzzle

Activity: Puzzles stimulate children's thinking skills. Stop your world and become a part of your child's world for just five minutes. Work a puzzle together. Enjoy your child's facial expressions and the way she moves her tongue while thinking and placing the puzzle pieces.

Words such as "way to go," "you're awesome," and "you did that so well" help build self-esteem.

Thank your child for putting away the puzzle when you're done.

A Minute for Mom: *Blessing our children means understanding their unique bent.*—Gary Smalley and John Trent, *The Blessing*

It's Not a Puzzle Anymore

Activity: On one of your child's *cardboard* puzzles, print consecutive numbers with a permanent marker on the back of each puzzle piece, starting with the number one. (Use only one number on each puzzle piece.)

In the frame holder of the puzzle, copy the exact same number on each piece of the puzzle that *matches* the shape outline on the card-board frame.

Now your child can put the puzzle pieces together by matching numbers.

Materials:
A child's cardboard puzzle

Week Twenty-Five: Parts of the Puzzle

A Minute for Mom: *Reflect upon your present blessings, of which every man has many: not on your past misfortunes, of which all men have some.*—Charles Dickens

My Family Puzzle

Materials:
A duplicate family snap-shot

Activity: One day, when you get double prints on a roll of film from a family event, take two matching pictures and create a personal puzzle for your child.

Cut up one picture into about five large sections. Then let your child try to put the picture pieces together while *looking* at the uncut matching picture.

Have your child put all the pieces into a zip-lock bag and find a special place for it in his room.

Journal thoughts to remember...

A Minute for Mom: *Dear God, my days seem so hectic sometimes. Please help me set priorities that please you.*

Author! Author!

Activity: Help your child make an "I Can" book. Fold two pieces of paper in half and staple on the folded side. Talk about things she can do such as share her toys, give great hugs, and love Jesus. Ask her to think of other things she can do.

Explain that sometimes we do things quickly, but today the two of you are going to make a book that she'll want to "save forever" if she takes her time. Tell her it will take three days to make the book.

Make the title page by printing "I Can" and the word "by." Help your child print her name because she will be the author and illustrator! On page one, print the words of one thing your child said she could do. Let your child illustrate it. Then put the book in a large zip-lock bag to keep it clean as though it were a priceless treasure (and it will be!).

Materials:
Two plain sheets of paper 8.5 x 11 in.

Crayons or colored markers

Stapler (help your child use this tool)

day 2

A Minute for Mom: *Richer than I you can never be, I had a mother who read to me.*—Strickland Gillilan

See What I Can Do

Materials:

The "I Can" book

Crayons or colored markers

Activity: Take out the book your child is making entitled, "I Can." Hold your child on your lap and read the first page with her. Thank your child for taking her time. (Children's drawings are sometimes hard to understand, but continue to smile if you don't know what something is because *your child will be watching your face to see if you enjoy her work.*)

Discuss some other things your child can do. Choose one and print the words on page two. While your child illustrates this word, sit down next to her and enjoy the moment together.

A Minute for Mom: *Dear God, as I lay in bed, I sometimes think back over my day and wonder, did my child see you in me? Please renew your love in me and help me be a good mother.*

My "I Can" Book

Activity: Find a comfortable chair, hold your child, and read the "I Can" book with him. Then print the words your child wants on the third page of the book. While he is coloring the third page, decorate a little box for the book to fit in. You could even glue a small picture of your child on the title page so everyone can see the author! (If you don't have a small box, the large zip-lock bag should keep it clean.)

After your child shares the book with family and friends, save it as a precious childhood treasure you made together.

Journal thoughts to remember...

Materials:
The "I Can" book

Crayons or colored markers

A small box

A Minute for Mom: *Truth, which is important to a scholar, has got to be concrete. And there is nothing more concrete than dealing with babies, burps and bottles, frogs and mud.*
—Jeane J. Kirkpatrick

Look What I Found

Activity: Give your child a zip-lock bag to collect ten rocks of various sizes from your yard.

Together, lay the rocks out on the floor and enjoy their beauty. Mention how wonderful it was for God to create the world with rocks for us to enjoy. Then talk about their color, size, sparkles, smoothness, and points.

Ask your child to sort the rocks into three piles by size (small, medium, and large). Lay them in a line to see which row has the most, the least, or the same. (Make sure your child counts slowly as she counts each rock.)

Try sorting the rocks into two piles by light and dark colors, or smooth and rough. Put the rocks in a zip-lock bag for another day.

A Minute for Mom: *My God is my rock.*—2 Samuel 22:3

God Is My Rock!

Activity: Give the bag of rocks to your child. Ask your child to pick out one of the biggest rocks and hold it in his hand. Ask him if the rock is soft or if it can move away. Discuss how a rock is solid and doesn't move.

Materials:
Bag of rocks from day one

Tell your child that God is just like that rock. He's solid and will never move away from us. Mention that a lot of things in life break and fall apart, such as toys and cars, but God is always there for each of us. Put the rock your child chose on a shelf in his room. Whenever your child is afraid, tell him to remember that God is our rock and He will help him. During bedtime prayers, thank God for always being with us.

Check at the library for picture books on rocks. (Save the big bag of rocks for Day 3.)

day
3

A Minute for Mom: *Dear God, help me to be a rock to my child like you are a rock to me—always there to listen and always there to help.*

I'm a Rock Sorter!

Materials:
The zip-lock bag of rocks (from week Twenty-Seven, Day 1)

A shoe box with lid

A knife

A marker

Activity: Make a rock sorter for your child.

Take a shoe box lid and cut three different-sized holes (small, medium, and large). Keep in mind the size of the rocks collected earlier, so you don't cut the holes too big. Print the words "small," "medium," and "large" on top of the lid, under the appropriate holes.

Mention that someone who finds rocks interesting is called a "rock hound."

Journal thoughts to remember...

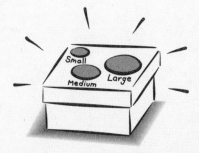

A Minute for Mom: *To us as parents is entrusted the vital task of character development—of imprinting the distinctive stamp of godliness upon the lives of our children.*—Maxine Hancock

Please See Me When I'm Good

Activity: So often, when a child is being good, his behavior goes unnoticed. It's when a child is bad that he usually gets our attention.

Materials:
Observant
eyes

Today, make an effort to observe your child doing something good. For example, being kind while playing with a friend, picking up his toys, waiting patiently for something, or doing other kind acts.

Thank your child, then ask him how he felt acting in a kind way.

Work to catch your child in the act of doing good things and thank him with words, hugs, and kisses!

Kindness, when reinforced, will bring about even greater kindness!

day

2

A Minute for Mom: *I can do everything through him who gives me strength.*—Philippians 4:13

Please Listen, Mom

Materials:
A mom
who listens

Activity: Another way to build your child's self-esteem is to be a better listener when she talks to you.

Think about it. How do you feel when you talk to someone and they *don't look* or *listen* to you? Or maybe the person listens somewhat but is busy doing other things. Do you feel respected in that situation? Worthwhile?

Try to make it a point today to *really look* at your child when she talks to you. Better yet, kneel down, look into her eyes, and just listen.

It sounds simple, but it's not easy because we are so busy. Listening to your child builds her self-esteem because you are showing her your love.

A Minute for Mom: *Be kind and compassionate to one another, forgiving each other, just as in Christ, God forgave you.* —Ephesians 4:32

Always Love

Activity: It is important for your child to realize that everyone makes mistakes and that no one is perfect.

While tucking your child into bed, tell him about a time when you were young and made a mistake. Talk about your feelings. Hopefully, you learned something from the experience and your parents forgave you.

Tell your child you will always love him and you don't expect him to be perfect—just to try hard to do good. Talk about how Christ lived. He is our example.

Journal thoughts to remember…

Materials:
An understanding mom

A Minute for Mom: *I am sure that if people had to choose between living where the noise of children never stopped, and where it was never heard, all the good natures and sound people would prefer the incessant noise to the incessant silence.*—George Bernard Shaw

I Can Be an Astronaut!

Materials:

A one gallon plastic milk carton

Colored paper

Markers

Tape

A blanket

Activity: Most children love to wear hats. Tell your child you're going to make a hat together. Talk about the type of "hat" people wear today if they live on a desert, in Mexico, etc.

Print the word "hat" and briefly mention that every letter has a name and a sound. If your child is interested, make the sound of "h," like the beginning of hat.

Here comes the fun! Cut off the entire top (two to three inches) of a one gallon milk carton. Then cut out the remaining handle section (approximately six by six inches).

This will be where your child's face shows. The *bottom* of the milk carton fits on the *top* of your child's head. Or simply use construction paper or newspaper and tape to create an interesting hat.

Let your child decorate it with crayons or markers. Create a spaceship by putting a blanket over a table. Now your child (and you, too, if you're game) can pretend to be an astronaut.

A Minute for Mom: *Dear God, help me not to get caught up in the mundane chores of life. Nudge me to take my child's hand, and let her lead me into her world.*

Sock It to 'Em

Activity: Using an old sock, give your child colored markers, buttons, scraps of fabric, and other items to create a "sock puppet."

First, print the word "sock" on a piece of paper and ask your child to touch the letter at the beginning of the word. Restate briefly that it is the letter "S" and it has a sound. Make the "S" sound as in the beginning of "sock."

Now get out all the recycled items for this activity and let your child create her own sock puppet.

Maybe your child would like to put on a puppet show for the family. Turning a card table on its side makes a great puppet theater.

Materials:

An old sock

Colored markers

Buttons

Fabric scraps

A Minute for Mom: *Love doesn't make the world go round. Love is what makes the ride worthwhile.*—Franklin P. Jones

Tubing with My Family

Materials:

Paper tubes of different lengths

Colored markers

Colored yarns

Activity: Ask your child what he thinks the word "family" means. Explain that some families have only a dad, some only a mother. Mention that some of the children in his kindergarten class may have a family that is made up differently than his. Point out that God loves all families.

Tell your child how thankful you are for your family and how much you love everyone in it. Now help your child create your family using paper tubes of different lengths. (A paper tube for each member of the family.)

Decorate the tubes with faces, hair, clothing, etc. to represent your family. Display them as a center-piece for dinner!

Journal thoughts to remember…

A Minute for Mom: *You never know what small act of love and encouragement will be the one that your children remember as a key way in which you blessed them.* —Gary Smalley and John Trent, *The Blessing*

Sound It Out!

Activity: Print the capital first letter of your child's name on a piece of paper. Have him tell you the name of the letter. Ask him to notice some other things about that letter: Does it have a straight line? Is it pretty? Thank him for being such a good "thinker."

    Tell your child the letter also has a sound. Make the sound of the first letter in your child's first name. Have him make the identical sound. Think of another word that begins with the sound of your child's name and say it. Ask him if he can hear that both words start with the same sound. (Children need a lot of repetition until they learn something, so be patient—this skill takes time.)

    Make a list together of words that start with the same sound and letter as your child's name. Ask your child to draw a line under all the first letters. Keep smiling—especially when you are teaching something new!

Materials:
Paper

Colored markers

Week Thirty: The Sound of *My* First Letter

A Minute for Mom: *Dear God, help me to be a mom who celebrates each step of growth my child makes, no matter how small.*

Learning with Playdough

Materials:
Playdough
from Week
11, Day 1

Activity: With playdough, have your child form the capital first letter in his name. You might have to print it for your child so he can see it.

Make the beginning sound of your child's name again and have your child make the same sound.

With your child, make objects out of the playdough that start with the same letter. For example, if your child's name starts with the letter "B," you and your child could make a ball, a basket, and a balloon. Remember to make this a fun activity.

A Minute for Mom: *The best portion of a good man's life, his little nameless, unremembered acts of kindness and of love.*
—William Wordsworth

I Know I'll Learn the Letter Sounds!

Activity: Teach this song to your child and sing it frequently around the house. Sing the words to the tune of "Oh, Do You Know the Muffin Man?"

Materials:
None

I know I'll learn the letter sounds,
the letter sounds,
the letter sounds.
I know I'll learn
the letter sounds,
And read by leaps and bounds!

Explain what the song means by "leaps and bounds."

Journal thoughts to remember…

Week Thirty-One: Shape Review

A Minute for Mom: *Pray as though everything depended on God. Work as though everything depended on you.*—St. Augustine

I'm Really Shaping Up!

Materials:
Colored
construction
paper and
scissors

Clear self-
stick paper

Magnetic strip

Crayons
or colored
markers

Activity: Using colored construction paper, cut out basic shapes (circle, square, triangle, rectangle, oval, diamond).

Let your child color each shape. As she completes a shape, cover it with clear self-stick paper, trim around the shape, and attach pieces of magnetic strip to the back.

Using your refrigerator or a metal baking sheet, play a game asking your child to do things with one shape at a time. For example, move the circle near the square, touch the shape that has three sides, point to the square, etc.

Keep the shapes on the refrigerator so you can review them frequently.

A Minute for Mom: *Laughter is inner jogging.*
—Norman Cousins

Shapes Are Everywhere!

Activity: Find a picture in a magazine that has lots of shapes in it. With your child on your lap, see if he can point out the shapes in the picture.

    Give clues and see if your child can name the object you are looking at in the picture. For example, tell him it's a circle, it's yellow, and it's hot. (The answer might be the sun.)

    If your child is enjoying the time together, let him choose a different picture and play the game again. (Let the dishes sit in the sink just a few minutes longer.)

Materials:
A magazine

Week Thirty-One: Shape Review

A Minute for Mom: *What one does is what counts and not what one had the intention of doing.*—Pablo Picasso

Shape Creation

Materials:
Construction paper of various colors

Glue and scissors

Activity: Using the construction paper, cut out three sizes of each of the basic shapes (circle, square, rectangle, triangle, oval, diamond). The largest shape should be no bigger than two to three inches.

Give your child a sheet of construction paper. (Your child's paper should not be the same color as the shapes.) Let her move the shapes around on the paper until she makes something with the shapes. (If your child can't make an object with the shapes, give her ideas, or just let her glue the shapes anywhere to make a collage!) Display the art prominently.

Journal thoughts to remember…

A Minute for Mom: *Therefore, as God's chosen people, holy and dearly loved, clothe yourselves with compassion, kindness, humility, gentleness and patience.*—Colossians 3:12

Look What I Made!

Activity: Using an empty tissue box that has an oval cutout on the top, create a cute picture frame. Let your child draw a picture for the frame. Trace around the oval on a plain piece of paper so your child knows the size of the oval before he draws a picture.

Cut around the perimeter of the top of the tissue box so the oval is in the middle. Let your child smooth liquid glue over the top of the box. Next, sprinkle rice over the glued area. (This time, use more than just a little so the rice adheres.) Discuss the oval shape. Let it dry completely.

Attach your child's drawing to the completed frame. Together, decide where to hang it.

Materials:

A tissue box with an oval cutout on the top

Scissors and liquid glue

A sheet of white paper

One cup of dry rice

Crayons or colored markers

day 2

A Minute for Mom: *Into the woman's keeping is committed the destiny of the generations to come after us.*—Theodore Roosevelt

I Can Pour!

Materials:
About nine pounds of dry rice or bird seed

A plastic tray or dish pan, approximately twelve by twelve inches

Plastic containers, pitchers, measuring spoons, funnels, scoops, etc.

Activity: Pour the rice into a tray or dishpan. Let your child explore measuring and pouring skills with measuring spoons, plastic salad dressing containers, funnels, scoops, a small pitcher, and other small plastic containers.

She will find hours of enjoyment playing and learning with the rice. Teach your child how to clean up her mess before playing with another toy. (You might want this to be an outside activity.)

A Minute for Mom: *The one thing children wear out faster than shoes is parents.*—John J. Plomp

Please Bag It, Mom

Activity: Like bean bags, rice bags make wonderful, inexpensive toys for children. Here's how to make a quick rice bag.

    Cut out a pocket from an old blouse, dress, pants, or jacket. Include the fabric the pocket is attached to, leaving a little material beyond the stitching. Let your child fill the opening with rice. Sew up the open end for your child.

    Practice tossing the rice bag into a box or paper bag. Play toss or catch or dance with the rice bag.

Journal thoughts to remember…

Materials:
About a cup
of dry rice

A pocket from
an old blouse,
dress, pants
or jacket

Thread and
needle

Week Thirty-Three: I Know How to Lace

A Minute for Mom: *Indeed, I owe to [my mother's] loving wisdom all that was bright and good in my long night.*—Helen Keller

Lace It Up

Materials:

A five- or six-inch plain paper plate

Hole puncher

A piece of yarn about twenty-five inches long

Liquid glue

Optional: glitter, cereal, dried parsley

Activities: Using a small white paper plate, punch holes around the perimeter. Holes should be about one and a half inches apart. Tape one end of the yarn onto the *back* of the plate. Using the other end of the yarn, show your child how to come from *under* the plate and *pull* the yarn *up*. Then insert the yarn into the next hole and *push* the yarn *down*. Sing this song to the tune of "Mary Had a Little Lamb":

Pull the yarn up
through the hole,
through the hole,
through the hole,
Pull the yarn up
through the hole,
Then under to the next.

When lacing is completed, print the first letter of your child's name in the center with liquid glue. Let your child cover the glue with glitter, crumpled cereal, parsley, etc.

A Minute for Mom: *There is a net of love by which you can catch souls.*—Mother Teresa

Lacing Straws

Activities: Cut two different-colored plastic straws into about one-inch segments. Separate the colors by placing them in different containers.

Review what an AB pattern is with your child (an alternating pattern). For example, wiggle, stop, wiggle, stop; or stand, sit, stand, sit. Show her how to lace the straws and create a pattern of alternating colors.

To get your child started, fold over a piece of tape on one end of the yarn so the straw pieces stop and don't fall to the ground when they are added. Wrap the other end of the yarn with about a half-inch of tape to make lacing easier. Then watch your child to see if she understands an AB pattern.

When finished, tie the ends together so your child can wear the necklace. *Give her a hug.*

Materials:
Two different colored plastic straws

A piece of yarn about twenty-four inches long

Tape

A Minute for Mom: *Dear God, I am beginning to feel that our world has raised more children who "want" than children who "give." Help my child learn the importance of "giving back" to society.*

A Sweet-Heart

Materials:
Red construction paper

Hole puncher

A piece of candy

A piece of yarn about two feet long

Activities: Thoughtfulness is a wonderful quality to instill in your child. Here's how to help him make a surprise gift. Help your child fold and cut out two identical hearts from red construction paper. Hold them together and hole-punch around the perimeter, leaving about one and a half inches between holes. Tape the top and bottom together so it will be easier to lace. (Follow lacing instructions from Week 33, Day 1.)

When finished, remove the tape and fill the heart with a piece of candy. Together place it under someone's pillow.

Journal thoughts to remember…

A Minute for Mom: *Dear God, I think about the words "In the beginning…" and then I think about my child's beginning. May these years be filled with patience, my gentle voice, and overflowing love.*

Two Letters in My Name!

Activities: On a notepad, without your child seeing you, press down firmly with a pencil and print the first two letters in your child's name (only the first one is a capital). Now tear off the sheet of paper and throw it away.

Give your child a dark crayon. Tell her there are two very important things on this blank piece of paper. To discover what they are, your child has to move the crayon firmly back and forth across the paper.

Magic! Two important letters appear! Discuss the name of each letter. Then take your child's finger and trace over the letters, as your child says the name of each letter.

Materials:
A blank notepad

Pencil

Crayons

day 2

A Minute for Mom: *Only mothers can think of the future—because they give birth to it in their children.*—Maxim Gorky

Buried Treasure

Materials:

A bag of popcorn

Two jar lids

Magnetic strip

Dark permanent marker

Activities: Wash two jar lids. With a permanent marker, print the first two letters in your child's name, one letter in each lid. (The first letter should be capital, the second lowercase.) Put a piece of magnetic strip on the back of each lid. Then bury the lids in a bag of popcorn!

Tell your child there is something very important buried in the popcorn. After she washes her hands carefully, let her try to find the buried treasure.

Once your child finds the lids, have her put them on the refrigerator in the proper order. Praise her for a job well done.

A Minute for Mom: *When God thought of mother, He must have laughed with satisfaction, and framed it quickly—so rich, so deep, so divine, so full of soul, power, and beauty was the conception.*
—Henry Ward Beecher

Sing It Out!

Activities: Review the first letter of your child's first and last name. Teach your child the following words to the tune of "Ten Little Indians."

Materials: None

> I can say my first two letters,
> I can say my first two letters,
> I can say my first two letters,
> They are_____and_____!

Then your child can sing to you:

> Do you know my first two letters,
> Do you know my first two letters,
> Do you know my first two letters?
> Tell me if you know.

Journal thoughts to remember...

day
I

A Minute for Mom: *The LORD God formed the man from the dust of the ground—Genesis 2:7*

Comparing Soil

Materials:

Three plastic sandwich bags

A small shovel or scoop

Three plastic meat trays

Activities: Use three plastic sandwich bags and perhaps a small shovel or scoop, to collect samples of soil as you go for a walk with your child.

While walking, try to collect different types of dirt. Discuss how the words "soil" and "dirt" mean the same thing. You might review the beginning sounds of "dirt" and "soil."

Ask your child why he thinks God made dirt. *Look* at your child while he talks and give him a "one-minute" hug with your eyes.

When you return home, put the soils in three different plastic meat trays so your child can examine them. Discuss texture, color, objects in the soil, and what dirt is made from.

day

2

A Minute for Mom: *A picture memory brings to me:*
I look across the years and see myself beside my mother's knees.
—John Greenleaf Whittier

I Like Mud!

Activities: Have your child put on old clothes. Get a bucket half-full of sand. Outside, let him pour water in it until he likes the consistency of the "mud."

Give your child plastic containers (margarine, yogurt, etc.) to make a sand castle. Show him how to mold the wet sand.

During bedtime prayers, thank God for giving us so much to enjoy on the earth.

Materials:
Old clothing for your child to wear

A half-full bucket of sand

Water

Plastic containers

day 3

A Minute for Mom: *A house without love may be a castle or a palace, but it is not a home.*—John Lubbock

"Dirt Cheap" Treat

Materials:
One small zip-lock bag

Three chocolate sandwhich cookies

Rolling pin

Optional: gummy worm

Activities: In a small zip-lock bag, have your child crush the cookies with a rolling pin or by hand. (Make sure the bag is sealed to keep the crushed cookies inside the bag.)

Put the crushed cookies in a cup. Then give your child a spoon and a gummy worm. Now your child can pretend he is eating dirt! Talk *briefly* about the beginning sounds of the words "dirt," "worm," and "gummy." (You could invite a friend over to enjoy eating "dirt" with your child.)

Journal thoughts to remember...

A Minute for Mom: *If you have faith as small as a mustard seed, you can say to this mountain, "Move from here to there" and it will move. Nothing will be impossible for you.*—Matthew 17:20

A Little Faith Is Powerful!

Activities: Visit the local nursery or walk around your neighborhood. Point out to your child all the plants that came from seeds and explain to her that seeds are small miracles. Tell your child that her faith in God only needs to be as big as a mustard seed! To visually show her that size, find a tiny button and say that a mustard seed is smaller than the button. (Real mustard seeds would be a better example.)

Discuss how a seed can grow very tall with just the right amount of sunlight, water, and loving care.

Find a sunny spot in your yard for your child to plant sunflower seeds or another plant that thrives in your area. Teach her to water the plants when needed and to pull weeds that grow around it.

She will be amazed at how large it will grow. Point out how a little faith—the size of a mustard seed—is *powerful!*

Materials:
Sunflower seeds (or seeds from a plant that grows tall in your area)

Optional: mustard seed

Pulling Weeds

Materials:
A trip to a local nursery or garden supply store

A hoe

Activities: Make it a point to visit a garden shop so your child can see all the things related to planting. If you can't do that, find a hoe to use for teaching this activity.

Show your child a hoe. Discuss what it is used for. Mention that it gets rid of the weeds so the plant can grow better.

Explain that, just like plants, we grow every day and should try to be kind like Christ and get rid of our bad actions.

Tell your child that in a way, we are getting rid of our weeds when we grow in love and try to be like him.

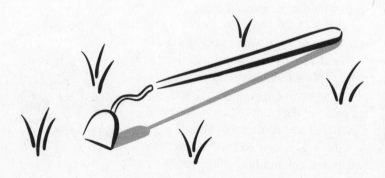

A Minute for Mom: *This is my command: Love each other.*
—John 15:17

Love Grows

Activities: Show your child a simple illustration about how love grows by blowing up a balloon.

Materials:
A balloon

Blow a little air into a balloon and tightly pinch the end. Tell your child that love is like a balloon. Blow more air into it, stop, and ask your child what is happening to the balloon. He might say it's growing or it's getting bigger. Mention that God wants our love to grow and grow and *grow!* Continue blowing up the balloon but do not pop it. Tie a knot in it and let your child bounce it into the air.

At bedtime, talk about ways his love can grow (such as being nice to his brother or sister, or helping a friend.)

Journal thoughts to remember…

day

1

A Minute for Mom: *Enjoy the little things, for one day you may look back and realize they were the big things.*—Robert Brault

Stop and Listen

Materials:
An empty adult-size shoe box or another similar-sized box

Activities: Using an empty box, have your child perform a "shoe box" dance while following your directions. For example, ask her to jump over the box, put one foot in the box, stand next to the box, etc. Let your child be the teacher and give you directions for the dance, too.

Thank your child for being a good listener and following directions. Mention that her kindergarten teacher will be thankful to see how hard she tries to be a good listener.

A Minute for Mom: *Most people are about as happy as they make up their minds to be.*—Abraham Lincoln

Words, Words, Words

Activities: Using an old catalogue or magazine, let your child cut out two toys or interesting objects. Place the cut-out objects face up on the construction paper for a "follow-the-directions" game.

Before giving directions, talk about what a corner is, what the word "beside" means, and where the top, bottom, and middle of the paper are. Now give directions about each toy (e.g.: "Place the truck in the middle of the paper." "Put it in a corner." "Put the two toys beside each other at the bottom.")

With a gentle voice, explain any directions your child *didn't* understand. *Keep smiling!*

Thank your child for being such a good listener.

Materials:
A piece of construction paper

Child-safe scissors

An old toy catalogue or magazine

day 3

A Minute for Mom: *Who ran to help me when I fell, And would some pretty story tell, Or kiss the place to make it well? My mother.*
—Ann Taylor

I Made My Own Sandwich

Materials:
Bread

Peanut butter
and jelly

Knife

Activities: Have your child make a peanut butter and jelly sandwich while you give him directions on how to make it.

For example, you might say, "First, get one piece of bread. Next, with a knife, spread a little peanut butter on the top of the bread." (Continue until your child has made his own sandwich.) Your child will be proud of his accomplishment.

Don't forget, your child is capable of cleaning up the mess! Break the cleanup into small steps.
First, close all the jars.
Next, take them "back home" where they belong.

Journal thoughts to remember…

A Minute for Mom: *He who laughs, lasts!*
—Mary Pettibone Poole

Yum! Yum!

Materials:
Straight
pretzels

Activities: Print your child's first name on a piece of paper
(capitalizing the first letter only). If you'd like to, you may cover
the paper with clear adhesive paper for protection.

A plain piece
of paper,
approximately
three by ten
inches

On the paper with your child's name printed on it, have
her lay straight pretzels to cover each letter. Some of the pretzels
may have to be broken for curved letters. Your child may eat
the pretzels after each letter is copied.

Eat up and enjoy!

(Save the paper and use it for the following two days'
activities.)

Colored
markers or
crayons

Optional:
clear adhesive
paper (usually
near contact
paper in
stores)

day 2

A Minute for Mom: *If we make our goal to live a life of compassion and unconditional love, then the world will indeed become a garden where all kinds of flowers can bloom and grow.*
—Elisabeth Kubler-Ross

Materials:
Your child's printed name from Week 38, Day 1

Two strips of plain paper, approximately three by ten inches long

Crayons or colored markers

Comparing Names

Activities: Have your child look at his name on the piece of paper and count the letters in his name.

Now print your first name on a strip of paper (using the same letter size in which you printed your child's name) and lay it above his name.

Let your child look at both names. Then ask if there is anything interesting about the names. Do any letters look alike? Whose name is longer? Shorter? Or equal?

Print Jesus' name on a piece of paper using the same letter size in which you printed your name. Lay it above the other names. Which name is longer now?

A Minute for Mom: *Love is the chain whereby to bind a child to his parents.*—Abraham Lincoln

I Love My Name

Activities: As your child studies the paper with her name printed on it, ask her different questions about her name. Where is the beginning of her name? Where is the end? (Knowing where to locate the beginning of a word is a very important concept in learning to read.) Does your child know any of the letters' names?

Give your child a bowl of dry cereal. Let her cover each letter of her name with pieces of cereal. Be sure your child starts at the beginning of her name, going from left to right.

Journal thoughts to remember…

Materials:
Your child's printed name from Week 38, Day 1

One cup of dry cereal

Week Thirty-Nine: Math with Trash

A Minute for Mom: *Dear Father God, thank you that I can count on you. Please help me to be the kind of mother my child can always count on!*

Estimate? I Guess!

Materials:
Twelve empty aluminum cans (with no sharp edges) or cardboard frozen juice cans

A sheet of paper

Crayons or colored markers

Activities: Work on estimation (guessing). Have your child guess how many empty aluminum cans he will be able to stack up, one on top of the other.

Count each can with your child as he adds each one to the top of the stack. On a sheet of paper, print numbers one through twelve in a line. *Circle* the total number stacked each time your child tries it.

When finished, your child will be able to see, on the number line you made, which number was the highest!

Toss It Here

Activities: Make and play a game called "Yogurt Toss." Give your child a clean, empty yogurt container and a small object, such as a ball or walnut. Tell him to toss the object into the air and try to catch it with the yogurt container. (Make sure he is careful not to let the object hit his face.)

    Each time your child catches the object, make a small straight line on a piece of paper. Tally by fives. After drawing four straight lines, make a diagonal line through the four lines to represent the number five.. Explain to him that this is a way to count by fives.

Materials:

A clean, empty yogurt container

A ping pong ball or small soft ball

Scratch paper and pencil

day 3

A Minute for Mom: *Dear God, I like to be around people who are fun to be with. I never thought about it until now, but my child probably likes to be around people who are fun, too! Please help me to be fun!*

I'm a Builder

Materials:
Clean, empty cans with no sharp edges

Optional: Colored tape or contact paper

Activities: Clean, empty cans of different sizes with no sharp edges make great building and stacking toys. You could even color the outsides of the cans with colored tape or contact paper.

Play the "copy cat" game. You build an easy pyramid first and let your child try to copy yours. Next, challenge your child by making a harder one. Build a giant tower together.

When you're done, find a ball and try bowling together!

Journal thoughts to remember…

A Minute for Mom: *The eggs do not teach the hen.*
—Russian Proverb

I Can Play Basketball

Activities: Make a basketball game together. Help your child crumple five sheets of newspaper into tight, individual balls. Tape could be applied to the newspaper balls to keep the paper together.

Get an empty wastebasket or box. Put a piece of tape on the floor to designate where your child should stand to play the game. Place the wastebasket about three feet from the tape line. Have your child stand on the tape and try to throw each paper ball into the box.

You play, too!

Materials:

Empty waste-
basket or box

Newspaper

Masking tape

A Minute for Mom: *One person can make a difference and every person should try.*—John F. Kennedy

Making a Match

Materials:

Two date pages from an old calendar

Adult scissors and child-safe scissors

Zip-lock bag

Activities: Using the numbers from two pages of a calendar, have your child cut out numbered squares one through ten. You cut out a *matching* set of numbers, too.

Randomly lay the numbers face down on a table in rows of four or five. Play a concentration game with your child (sometimes called "Memory"). Each of you turn over two numbers at a time and try to get a match.

If this activity is too hard for your child, use numbers one through five for a while.

When you are done, give your child a zip-lock bag to keep the numbers in and play the game another day.

A Minute for Mom: *Dear God, today my child said to me in a sincere voice, "Mommy, can you hear good? I've been calling and calling you to see the blocks I made." Please help me not to be so consumed by my world.*

A Super Sculpture!

Activities: When you clean out your pantry and find old marshmallows or raisins, don't throw them away. Instead, use them for your child to make a sculpture.

Encourage your child to build a sculpture simply by poking a marshmallow or raisin with a toothpick. Add another marshmallow or raisin to the other end of the toothpick and keep going! If your child's structure collapses, encourage him to try again. Just say, "That's okay. That happens sometimes."

Journal thoughts to remember…

Materials:
Old marshmallows or raisins (this activity is easier to do if they are dried out a little)

A box of toothpicks

day 1

A Minute for Mom: *That which you cannot give away, you do not possess. It possesses you.*—Ivern Ball

A "Fair Share"

Materials:
Playdough
from Week
11, Day 1

Activities: Tell your child you're going to play school with him. Give him *all* the playdough. Pretend you are a new friend and ask your child for some playdough. See if he gives you a "fair share." Thank him if he does and express your feelings.

Now *you* take all the playdough and say, "What if I only gave you a *tiny bit* of playdough and I kept all the rest? (Put a little playdough in your child's hand.) How would you feel? Is it fair? Instead of grabbing more, what could you say to me?" Mention that he might have a chance to play with playdough at school and it will be important to share. Discuss other ways to share at school and at home.

Thank your child for his good ideas. Mention that Jesus shared food, his time, and his love.

A Minute for Mom: *Oh, that we will realize the power of our words—both for good and bad: "The tongue has the power of life and death" [Proverbs 18:21]. If our tongues can be controlled, our mouths will be fountains of life, and we will be worth listening to.*
—Carole Mayhall

Sharing My Eyes and My Ears

Activities: Tell your child, "Let's play pretend." Pretend *not* to listen or look at your child when she is talking to you. Ask her how she felt when you weren't being friendly. (Your child might say "sad" or "left out.") Ask her how she thinks the kindergarten teacher would feel if the children didn't listen and look at the teacher when she was talking.

Materials: Time to discuss respect and feeling left out

Looking at and listening to other people when they are talking is a big part of respect. In a way, a person is "sharing" himself when he pays attention to someone.

Tell your child you are sorry if you forgot to listen to and look at her any time when she was talking. Plan to work on being good listeners.

day 3

Week Forty-One: Friendship Is Sharing

A Minute for Mom: *Dear God, sharing is sometimes hard for my child. Give me the right words to guide him from being "I" centered to "others" centered. And give me the desire to teach, because sometimes I'm just too tired.*

Friendly Discussion

Materials:
None

Activities: Look for opportunities in which your child can play with other children (in Sunday school, with neighbors, etc.). Notice him when he is being kind, friendly, and when he is sharing. Thank him.

During a quiet moment, talk about a time when your child was friendly with other children. Tell him that to have friends, a person must be friendly. Ask your child what it means to be friendly. Tell him the number of friends he will have depends on how he treats others. Mention that children enjoy being with someone kind.

Journal thoughts to remember…

A Minute for Mom: *I have been re-reading* Hudson Taylor's Spiritual Secret. *He discovered that being faithful is not as much in trying to be faithful, but in looking to the faithful One.*
—Carole Mayhall

What's a Space, Mom?

Activities: Have your child stand up and put her feet close together. Ask her if there is a space between her feet. (No.) Now ask her to move her feet apart to create a space.

Mention that when she learns to read, there will be a space between every word on every page in the book.

Show your child what her name would look like if you printed it three times without any spaces in between. Now print her name three times with a space between each word.

Surprise your child and say, "Right now I don't want any space between us." Pause so your child can think about what you said, and then give her a *hug!*

Materials:
A plain sheet of paper

A pencil and crayon

Week Forty-Two: Reading Readiness

A Minute for Mom: *Dear God, patience, patience, patience…time, time, time! I need more of both, so please mold me to be like you.*

Where Do I Begin?

Materials:
One of your child's favorite books

Activities: Read one of your child's favorite books to him.

When you are done, ask him where the beginning of the book is located. See if he can find the first word on the first page.

Can your child touch the first word on the second page? Give him a *big* smile if he can! If not, give him a *big* smile anyway, and teach your child where to find the first word on two more pages.

Let your child be the teacher and ask you to find the first, second, or third word on a page.

Pick your child up and say, "You're awesome, and I love you."

A Minute for Mom: *If you cannot lift the load off another's back, do not walk away. Try to lighten it.*—Tyger

Why Do Books Have Dots?

Activities: Read one of your child's favorite books. When you finish, ask your child if she sees anything on a page that's interesting. Be encouraging of all her responses.

Materials:
One of your child's favorite books

Then point out the periods at the end of every sentence. Explain that this means "the end of a thought" and that it works like a stop sign.

Say to your child, "I love you." Tell her that if you printed the words on a piece of paper, you would make a dot at the end which is called a "period." Now write out "I love you" and show your child on paper! Look through a magazine and put a dot of color with a marker on all the periods your child can find.

A piece of paper, approximately three by five inches

Journal thoughts to remember…

day

1

A Minute for Mom: *I value this delicious home feeling as one of the choicest gifts a parent can bestow.*—Washington Irving

Eating in the Cupboard

Materials:
A plain piece of paper, eight and a half by eleven inches

Pencil

A handful of dry food (e.g., raisins, dry cereal, small crackers)

Optional: clear adhesive paper

Activities: Make the game called "eating in the cupboard." On a piece of plain paper draw two horizontal lines to divide the paper into three equal parts. Tell your child to pretend these spaces are shelves in the cupboard. (Cover the paper with clear adhesive paper and play often.)

Give your child a handful of food. Tell him to put one raisin on the top shelf and one raisin on the middle shelf. Ask your child to now *move* the raisins to the *bottom* of the cupboard so he can reach them. Ask how many there are. Review the example by saying one plus one equals two. *Eat up!*

Play this game for about five minutes and put no more than three pieces of food on a shelf.

A Minute for Mom: *And we urge you,...help the weak, be patient with everyone.*—1 Thessalonians 5:14

Adding with Numbers!

Activities: Make the following problems on separate three-by-five cards:

1 + 1 =
1 + 2 =
1 + 0 =
2 + 2 =

Show the flash card "1 + 1 =" to your child. Ask her what she sees. Is anything interesting? Tell your child that when you played "eating in the cupboard" this is how the game looks with numbers on a piece of paper.

Give your child the paper with the "pretend cupboard" and *slowly* help your child use food to work the problem.

Try the other flash cards but keep the game short and sweet!

Materials:
Four three-by-five index cards

Dark-colored marker

A handful of dry food (cereal, raisins, small crackers)

The "pretend cupboard" paper from Week 43, Day 1

Week Forty-Three: Eating and Adding

A Minute for Mom: *Love has nothing to do with what you are expecting to get, only what you are expecting to give.*
—Katharine Hepburn

My Turn to Be Teacher

Materials:
Math flash cards from Week 43, Day 2

"Pretend cupboard" paper from Week 43, Day 1

A handful of dry food (Cereal, raisins, small crackers)

Activities: Now you be the student and let your child be the teacher!

Give your child the flash cards you made. Get a handful of food and the "pretend cupboard" paper and say, "I'm ready, teacher!" to your child.

Pretend you don't know how to work a problem or two so your child has to be the teacher and help you. *Have fun!*

Journal thoughts to remember...

A Minute for Mom: *Dear God, help me to appreciate more of the "little" things in life. Today I came home from shopping and my child welcomed me with hugging arms. I'm so thankful to be a mother!*

The "Yummy" Take-Away Game

Activities: Put a cup of snack food in a dish near your child. Give your child a plain piece of paper. Tell her you are going to play the "take away" game together. Mention that it is called the "subtraction" game, too. Ask your child to count five pieces of food and lay them in a line on the piece of paper.

Tell your child a story: "Once upon a time there were five pieces of food. Along came a wonderful child and ate one!" (Have your child eat one.) Review what happened. Say, "You had five and ate one. How many do you have left? (Four.) Pause and say, "Five take away one equals four."

Continue to play the game. Each time, have your child subtract one and tell you how many are left until all five pieces are gone.

Materials:
A plain piece of paper, eight and a half by eleven inches or smaller

A handful of dry food (cereal, raisins, small crackers)

Week Forty-Four: Fun with Subtracting

A Minute for Mom: *After the verb "to love," the verb "to help" is the most beautiful verb in the world.*—Bertha Von Suttner

Where Did They Go?

Materials:
A plain piece of paper, five by eight inches, with a subtraction sign (-) in the middle

Five small toys (your child's preference)

Activities: Have your child get five small toys and lay them in a line on the floor.

Hold up the take-away sign (-) and tell him that together you are going to play a subtraction game and this line means "to take away."

Ask your child if he remembers what it means to subtract or take away. (Review this with him if needed before you play the game today.)

Hold the subtraction sign up for your child to see. Have him pretend to draw the same kind of line in the air. Now ask your child to count the toys and then take one away by placing it behind him. Ask, "How many are left?" Review by saying, "Five take away one equals four."

Continue to play until all five toys have been taken away.

day
3

A Minute for Mom: *Those who are lifting the world upward and onward are those who encourage more than criticize.*
—Elizabeth Harrison

I Love Playing Games

Activities: Place a bowl containing snack food beside your child. Tell your child to count five pieces of food and lay them in a line on the paper.

Decide whether or not you think your child needs to practice adding or subtracting with the food. Make up little stories such as, "A wonderful child was very hungry and ate one piece of food." (Your child should eat one.) "How many are left?"

Continue playing. Just remember to keep it short and fun!

Journal thoughts to remember...

Materials:
A plain piece of paper, eight and a half by eleven inches or smaller

Snack food (cereal, grapes, small cubes of cheese

Week Forty-Five: Fun as a Family

A Minute for Mom: *Dear God, I am so thankful you are at the core of my being. I pray that my child will someday feel the same way. Help me light her way just as my mother did for me.*

A Candlelight Dinner

Materials:
Food for dinner

Candle and matches

Activities: Let your child help plan a surprise candlelight dinner for the family. Even if hot dogs are served, candlelight makes it more enjoyable and cozy. You may want to invite grandparents or another special guest.

Make a list of food items to purchase and go shopping together. Let your child help in other ways, such as setting the table or cleaning the kitchen.

This activity also helps teach thoughtfulness for others. During dinner, have family members tell what they admire about one another.

Appreciate being a family!

Week Forty-Five: Fun as a Family

A Minute for Mom: *The last of the human freedoms—to choose one's attitude in any given set of circumstances, to choose one's own way.*—Viktor Frankl

Hot Stuff!

Activities: Warming trays (for food) are a lot of fun for children but require supervision.

Cover a warming tray with foil. Place a piece of paper on the foil. Show your child the corners of the tray because it is not as hot there.

Each member of the family should experiment by placing a paper on top of the tray and then, by pressing down on the paper with a crayon, create a picture, letters, numbers, or shapes. The crayon will melt onto the paper! Lift each picture off to cool.

Materials:
Warming tray

Aluminum foil

Crayons without the paper around them

Construction paper

Week Forty-Five: Fun as a Family

A Minute for Mom: *Love is a great good that makes every heavy thing light. It is not burdened by the load it carries, and it sweetens the bitter.*—Thomas a' Kempis

"Chalk Talk"

Materials:
Chalk

Activities: On a nice day, have the family do "chalk talk" on the sidewalk!

Using chalk, outline each other's body on the driveway or sidewalk when it's not too hot. Everyone can then draw additional parts such as hair, clothes, eyes, etc.

Have fun!

Journal thoughts to remember...

A Minute for Mom: *God made two great lights—the greater light to govern the day and the lesser light to govern the night. He also made the stars.*—Genesis: 1:16

Starlight, Starbright

Materials:
An old blanket

A clear night

Activities: At night, get an old blanket and together, find an area in your yard to look at the stars. Lay there quietly with your child for awhile, just enjoying the presence of each other.

Ask your child who made the stars. Discuss what a gift they are from God. Tell her there are constellations in the sky. Explain that a constellation is an outline of stars showing something (for example, the little and big dippers). See if she can find the dippers.

Ask her why she thinks God made stars, or why God made the moon. (For light, beauty, etc.) During bedtime prayers thank God for the moon and the stars.

day 2

A Minute for Mom: *Dear God, my little child reached for my hand today as we walked together down our street. It was small and soft and felt so good. Is that how you feel when I hold your hand?*

Birds Need Me!

Materials:

A piece
of bread

A piece
of yarn,
approximately
eight inches
long

A star cookie
cutter

Activities: Using a star cookie cutter let your child cut a star out of a piece of bread.

   Tell your child that God wants us to shine like a star with kindness to others.

   With a small pencil, let your child put a hole in the bread near a tip on the star. Tie a piece of yarn to the star and help your child hang it on a tree branch for the birds to eat.

   Birds are part of God's fabulous creation!

A Minute for Mom: *Dear God, I feel so much better when I take time to think about you, play with my child, or laugh with a friend. Please help me to do all three things more often.*

A Sunny Day

Activities: On a sunny day, go outside and make shadows with your bodies. Have your child make a shadow as you draw around it with chalk. Have your child try to print his first name under the shadow outline. Play with your shadows. Try to play tag by jumping on each other's shadows. Talk about what causes shadows.

Journal thoughts to remember…

Materials:
A sunny day

Chalk
(optional)

Week Forty-Seven: Teaming Up

A Minute for Mom: *Dear God, sometimes I feel I do everything in the house! Help me to give more responsibility to each member in my family so I don't get so stressed! Thank you for the joy of watching my child "sparkle" as he learns.*

Sparkle Painting

Materials:

1/2 c. liquid starch

2 c. salt

Food coloring

Construction paper

Activities: Let your child be creative and try salt painting. Mix the starch, salt, and food coloring together. Show your child how to print his name. Then let him paint his name with salt paint.

Let him paint other designs, too. Show him how they sparkle in the sunlight after they dry.

A Minute for Mom: *It is a striking fact that Jesus never said a judgmental word to a repentant person. Rather, knowing what was in that person that might have caused a bad choice or the formation of an unrighteous value or a fear-driven panic, he simply said, "Here's my hand; let's start over."*—Gail MacDonald

Frame My Name

Activities: Your child will enjoy watercolor paints. Try something different. Have your child wet the entire piece of paper first with water and a brush. While the paper is wet, have her drop paint from a brush onto the paper. Cover the entire paper with colors.

Let the paper dry. Give your child a dark marker to print her name over the colored painting. Hang or display.

Materials:

Watercolor paint

Paint brush

White construction paper

Dark-colored marker

day 3

A Minute for Mom: *Dear God, when I start my day with you I always have a better day. Please give me the discipline to reach for you before I reach for my coffee.*

I'm Organized!

Materials:
None

Activities: Organization, organization, organization!

Each night before your child goes to bed, have him help you lay out his clothes for school the next day. *Everything* should be ready, including socks and shoes and backpack, if he has one. Permission slips and other forms need to be filled out the night before they are due. If you end up hurrying in the morning, it only adds to *your stress* and *your child's,* too.

Journal thoughts to remember…

A Minute for Mom: *We ponder God's withholding or bestowing and while we pine for what was never given and what was taken, today slips through our fingers.*—Teresa Burleson

I Have Goals Just Like Mom

Activities: Have your child climb into your lap. Ask her what she would like to learn in school. Maybe she will say she wants to learn how to read, or find out more about an interest of hers such as horses and dogs, or to make new friends.

Explain that these thoughts are your child's *goals*. Goals are thinking about what is important to learn or to do.

Share a goal of yours. Is it to be the best parent you can be? To be more like Jesus? To take a class and learn something new?

Briefly pray together about goals.

Materials:
None

Week Forty-Eight: Kindergarten Is Getting Close

A Minute for Mom: *Dear God, deciding what's important "this" day is something I need to think about when I wake. If I wait until night, I will have missed my chance. Please help me start my day by talking to you. I know you care.*

Rules Are to Help Us

Materials:
None

Activities: Ask your child if she has rules to obey. Discuss these rules. Ask the purpose for the rules. Then ask your child if the teacher and new friends in kindergarten will have any rules at school. Can your child guess what some of those rules might be?

Conclude by explaining to your child that rules help us to be safe and guide us to be kind.

A Minute for Mom: *I shall pass through this world but once. Any good, therefore, that I can do or any kindness that I can show to any human being let me do it now. Let me not defer or neglect it, for I shall not pass this way again.*—Anonymous

"What-If" Game

Activities: Play the "What-If" game. Ask your child some questions about "unexpected" school situations, and ask her how she would handle them.

Discuss these situations:

1. What would you do if you couldn't find any of your friends during recess on the playground and your class had left?
2. What would you do if you felt sick in the classroom?
3. What would you do if you didn't understand something?
4. What would you do if your friend wouldn't play with you?

Journal thoughts to remember…

Materials:
None

Week Forty-Nine: Two Weeks and Counting

A Minute for Mom: *Dear God, if I were starting a new job, I would be a little apprehensive wondering if I would be able to do the work and if I would make any new friends. My child will soon be starting a new "job." Help me do all I can to relieve my child's fears and replace that fear with trust in you.*

My School

Materials:
Time

Child's birth certificate

Immunization records

Activities: With your child, visit the school where he'll be attending. Stop by the school office to make sure you have filled out all the necessary papers. You'll probably need to show the office staff your child's birth certificate and immunization records.

Stop at the nurse's office and tell your child he may need to come here if he gets sick.

Introduce yourself to the principal if he or she isn't busy and introduce your child.

Locate your child's classroom, the bath-rooms, and the play-ground. Spend some time playing there!

A Minute for Mom: *Just do what must be done. This may not be happiness, but it is greatness.*—George Bernard Shaw

Clothes for School

Activities: Look for sales to purchase some clothes for your child. Remember, your child will be playing outside, painting, playing with playdough, and sitting and building on the floor at times, so she needs to wear comfortable rather than "fancy" clothing.

Materials:
Time to shop during sales!

Your child will probably need a sturdy, comfortable pair of tennis shoes to wear and a backpack to help organize things she will take to and from school.

During bedtime prayers, ask God to help your child's new teacher get ready for school, too!

Week Forty-Nine: Two Weeks and Counting

A Minute for Mom: *Life is either a daring adventure or nothing.*
—Helen Keller

I Know Where I'm Going!

Materials:
None

Activities: Visit your child's school again and go to the library. Meet the librarian if he is there. After enjoying some books together, see if your child can find his classroom. Look to see if there is a number on the door. Discuss the shape of the door.

Can your child find the bathrooms? If the child's school has a cafeteria, show it to him and mention that if there is a special program, he might go there to see it. Tell your child that children eat lunch in the cafeteria, too. Helping your child feel comfortable at school in new surroundings is important and reduces a lot of fear on the first day.

Journal thoughts to remember…

Week Fifty: One More Week, Great!

A Minute for Mom: *Dear God, it's hard to believe that in a few days I will be letting go of my child's hand on the first day of school. Please help my child and me hold tightly onto your hand when we are apart.*

Teaming Up

Activities: Together, plan a visit to your child's classroom to meet the teacher. Keep the meeting *brief*. Let the teacher know you are willing to help and ask if there are any materials that need to be put together or prepared. "Teaming up" will help your child be a winner!

Materials:
None

If your child will be riding a bus or will be picked up by a day-care van, check in the office to find out where she will be *arriving* and *leaving*. Then walk with her to that area so she gets familiar with where it is located.

In your prayers, ask God to help you and your child's teacher be a "team" so your child can have a successful school year!

day 2

A Minute for Mom: *For I know the plans I have for you,"* *declares the* LORD, *"plans to prosper you and not to harm you,* *plans to give you hope and a future."*—Jeremiah 29:11

I Can Print My Name

Materials:
Old clothes

Shaving cream

A sheet of paper,

Dark-colored marker

Activities: Have your child wear old clothes and get out the shaving cream.

Print your child's first name on a piece of paper. Have your child point to the beginning of her name and tell you the names of the letters she knows. Does she know the beginning sound of her name? Compliment her.

Holding on to your child's finger, help her trace all the letters in her name. Now let your child have fun printing her name in the shaving cream while looking at her name on the paper. How many letters can she print *without* looking at her printed name? Now let your child create other interesting things in the shaving cream.

Week Fifty: One More Week, Great!

A Minute for Mom: *Dear God, it's almost time for me to send my child to kindergarten. I have such mixed feelings…joy that my child is ready and excited to learn, but a part of me doesn't want this stage of his childhood to be over. Give me the strength to let go joyfully.*

It's Easy for Me!

Activities: Using playdough, see how many numbers your child can make from one through ten. Praise him for how many he knows! Show him how easy it is to make the number ten with playdough!

Compliment your child on being a hard worker and a good listener. Tell him that you can see he is ready for kindergarten!

Journal thoughts to remember…

Materials:
Playdough from Week 11, Day 1

Plan ahead: Purchase "glow stars" from a craft store (Will be needed for Week 51, Day 2.)

day

1

Week Fifty-One: The Night Before School

A Minute for Mom: *Dear God, my child is so precious to me. Thank you for making motherhood possible. Please give me wisdom for each new step as my child grows. Help my child stand up to peer pressure as she grows older. Keep her close to you.*

Getting Ready

Materials:
The Book
*The Little
Engine That
Could*

Activities: In the evening, help your child lay out her back-pack and clothes in preparation for school tomorrow morning. Don't forget to include shoes and socks!

Hold your child in your lap. Give her a big hug, then a sincere "hug with your eyes" as you tell her wonderful things such as, "You can be so kind," or "You're a super listener. Your teacher is going to enjoy that quality about you."

Read the book *The Little Engine That Could.* Review how willing the engine was to help others. Then encourage your child to "try" hard like the little engine. Tell your child to say, *"I think I can!"* Ask your child if there is anything about school that she wants to talk or pray about.

A Minute for Mom: *Those who are wise will shine like the brightness of the heavens, and those who lead many to righteousness, like the stars for ever and ever.*—Daniel 12:3

I'm a Star!

Activities: Secretly attach your child's "glow stars" to his bedroom ceiling.

Materials:
"Glow stars" from craft store

During bedtime prayers, thank God for the words Jesus promised: "Never will I leave you." Ask God to be with your child and to help him in any way needed. Also thank God for your child's willingness to learn about being kind, and that he has such a good mind for learning.

Tell your child you have a surprise for him because he is such a "shining star." Turn off the lights in his room and have your child look at the ceiling to find his very own stars. Tell him that when he looks at the stars, he should thank God for making him so special. Then ask God to help him be a shining star at school.

Whisper "I love you" and say, "I'll see you in the morning, kindergartner. You're ready!"

day 3

A Minute for Mom: *I can do everything through him who gives me strength.*—Philippians 4:13

It's Time

Materials:
None

Activities: If possible, plan to meet with a friend tomorrow for coffee and a chat while your child is in school. At the very least, get in a phone call to air your feelings.

Tonight, slip into your child's bedroom while she is sleeping. Enjoy the peaceful quietness of the night.

Pray about tomorrow—a new beginning for her and you.

Embrace this time with joy because you have done your best to prepare her for this moment. Way to go, Mom! Now it is your turn to get some well-deserved rest and fall asleep with God's words on your heart, "Never will I leave you."

Journal thoughts to remember…

A Minute for Mom: *Dear God, here I am again knocking at your door asking you to watch over "our" child today. Thanks for loving us so much!*

Last-Minute Preparations

Activities: Make a circle button entitled, "I have courage." Print your child's name in the blank, cut it out, and attach ribbon streamers to make it look like a "first place" ribbon.

Safety-pin the button on your child's shirt before she goes to school (*If she wants to wear it!*). Explain what it says and that you are proud she is ready to go to kindergarten.

Materials:
Construction paper

Two ribbon streamers to attach to the button

day 2

A Minute for Mom: *Dear God, instill in me a love that helps my child want to someday change the world and be like you. Help me build a spiritual foundation in him that will provide strength to make a difference.*

Breakfast and Prayers with Mom

Materials:
A joyful heart!

Activities: Plan for plenty of time today to sit and have breakfast *with* your child. Before praying, ask your child what he would like God to do today for him while at school. Include your child's needs in your prayers.

An unhurried pace is best for such an important day! Take a picture of your child before taking him to school. If you can, take your child to school yourself on the first day and use your camera!

If your child will be eating lunch at school, give him packages of food that are easily opened. Also, tuck in a piece of candy or his favorite snack with a picture or a note that says "I love you."

Week Fifty-Two: My First Day of Kindergarten

A Minute for Mom: *He who dwells in the shelter of the Most High will rest in the shadow of the Almighty.*—Psalm 91:1

Activities: Spend some time writing down your thoughts. Then spend some well-earned quiet time in prayer and reading the Word. Congratulations on a job well done!

Journal thoughts to remember…

Alphabet Books
A, B, SEE!, Tana Hoban
A Is for Angry, Sandra Boynton
Alligators All Around, Maurice Sendak
Animalia, Graeme Base
Animals A to Z, David McPhail
Chicka Chicka ABC, Bill Martin Jr. & John Archambault
Clifford's ABC, Norman Bridwell
Dr. Seuss's ABC, Dr. Seuss

Basic Concepts
All About Where, Tana Hoban
Seven Blind Mice, Ed Young
Wheel Away, Dayle Ann Dodds
Where's Spot?, Eric Hill (enjoy other Spot books!)

Books for the Beginning of School
Arthur Goes to School, Marc Brown
Chrysanthemum, Kevin Henkes
Franklin Goes to School, Paulette Bourgeois
The Kissing Hand, Audrey Penn
Owen, Kevin Henkes
The Very Busy Spider, Eric Carle

Colors
A Color Clown Comes to Town, Jane Belk Moncure
Brown Bear, Brown Bear, Bill Martin, Jr.
Harold and the Purple Crayon, Crockett Johnson
Mouse Paint, Ellen Stoll Walsh
My Box of Color, Lorianne Siomades
My Crayons Talk, Patricia Hubbard

Counting
The Cheerios Counting Book 1-2-3, Barbara Barbieri McGrath
Count and See, Tana Hoban
The M & M's Counting Book, Barbara Barbieri McGrath
Moo Moo Brown Cow, Jakki Wood
One Two, One Pair, B. McMillan
Sea Squares, Joy N. Hulme
Ten Black Dots, Donald Crews

Death
Lifetimes, Bryan Mellonie and Robert Ingpen

Fairy Tales
Gingerbread Baby, Jan Brett
Goldilocks and the Three Bears, retold by Jan Brett
Jim Henson's Muppet Babies Big Book of Nursery Rhymes and Fairy Tales, illustrated by Lauren Attinello and Tom Brannon
The Gingerbread Man, retold by Eric A. Kimmel
The Little Red Hen

Folk Tales
The Enormous Turnip, illustrated by Kathy Parkenson
The Mitten, Jan Brett
Tikki Tikki Tembo, retold by Arlene Mosel

Kindness
Anna's Secret Friend, Yoriko Tsutsui
Just a Dream, Chris Van Allsburg
Miss Rumphius, Barbara Cooney
The Rainbow Fish, Marcus Pfister
Wilfrid Gordon McDonald Partridge, Mem Fox

Pattern Books
But I Can't Get My Turtle to Move, Elizabeth L. O'Donnell
Fortunately, Remy Charlip
"I Can't," Said the Ant, Polly Cameron
I Love Cats!, Catherine Matthias
Jump Frog Jump, Robert Kalan
Just Like Daddy, Frank Asch
Mouse's Birthday, Jane Yolen
The Napping House, Audrey Wood

Pure Enjoyment
Bently and Egg, William Joyce
Bunny Cakes, Rosemary Wells
Chicken Soup with Rice, Maurice Sendak
Clifford the Small Red Puppy, Norman Bridwell
Cookies Week, Cindy Ward
Corduroy, Don Freeman

Froggy Gets Dressed, Jonathan London
Goodnight Moon, Margaret Wise Brown
If You Give a Mouse a Cookie, Laura Joffe Numeroff
Many Zooms, Jane Cowen-Fletcher
Mooncake, Frank Asch
The Berenstain Bear series, Stan and Jan Berenstain
The Quilt Story, Tony Johnston and Tomie de
Paola
Town Mouse, Country Mouse, Jan Brett
Two Bad Ants, Chris Van Allsburg

Science
The Carrot Seed, Ruth Krauss
Chicken's Aren't the Only Ones, Ruth Heller
It's Pumpkin Time!, Zoe Hall
The Snowy Day, Ezra Jack Keats
Spiders, Gail Gibbons
Stellaluna, Janell Cannon
The Very Hungry Caterpillar, Eric Carle

Self-Esteem
I Like Me, Carlson
Jamaica's Find, Juanita Havill
The Very Quiet Cricket, Eric Carle

Sequence
Ox-Cart Man, Donald Hall
Pumpkin, Pumpkin, Jeanne Titherington

Sing While You Read
Shake My Sillies Out, (Raffi song)
Spider On the Floor, (Raffi song)
There Was an Old Lady Who Swallowed a Fly

MOTHERS OF

M♥PS®

PRESCHOOLERS

THE MOPS STORY

MOPS stands for Mothers of Preschoolers, a program designed for mothers with children under school age. These women come from different backgrounds and lifestyles yet have similar needs and a shared desire to be the best mothers they can be!

A MOPS group provides a caring, accepting atmosphere for today's mother of preschoolers. Here she has an opportunity to share concerns, explore areas of creativity, and hear instruction that equips her for the responsibilities of family and community. The MOPS program also includes MOPPETS, a loving, learning experience for children.

Approximately 2,500 groups meet in churches throughout the United States, Canada, and eleven other countries, to meet the needs of more than 100,000 women. Many more mothers are encouraged by the media arms of MOPS: *MomSense* radio and newsletter, MOPS' web site, and publications such as this book.

To receive information such as how to join a MOPS group, or how to receive other MOPS resources such as *MomSense* newsletter, call or write MOPS International, P.O. Box 102200, Denver, CO 80250-2200. Phone 1-800-929-1287. E-mail: Info@MOPS.org. Web site: www.MOPS.org. To learn how to start a MOPS group, call 1-888-910-MOPS. For MOPS products call The MOPS Shop at 1-888-545-4040.

About the Author

Sharon Wilkins has been an early childhood educator for more than 25 years. Her love of children includes many experiences: teacher, preschool director, staff development specialist, a nominee for Walt Disney's Teacher of the Year Award, writer of numerous articles, contributor to two books and a national speaker for parent/teacher workshops. Her philosophy of caring has touched thousands of lives. It is built on developing kinder, more capable children for our world. She and her family make their home in Arizona.

For more information on speaking and writing ministries, you may contact Wilkins at:

Sharon Wilkins
1157 W. Peninsula Dr.
Gilbert, AZ 85233
Phone: (480) 892-6684
Email: swilk44@aol.com

MOTHERS OF

M♥PS®

PRESCHOOLERS

Little Books for Busy Moms
Time Out for Mom ... Ahhh Moments

Beth Lagerborg, General Editor;
written by Cynthia W. Sumner

Every woman knows things she enjoys doing for herself, but having children can make nurturing yourself become more of a challenge. Activities or small indulgences of the past may no longer be possible due to time or financial limitations. At the same time, caring for your own needs is important for the well being of the family as a whole.

Time Out for Mom...Ahhh Moments gives you permission to indulge yourself from time to time—to let you know how valuable a little personal care can be for you and your family. Combining practical ideas on nurturing with personal experiences of mothers, this book encourages you to rekindle your love of self and rediscover your lost interests.

Softcover 0-310-23513-8

ZondervanPublishingHouse
Grand Rapids, Michigan

A Division of HarperCollinsPublishers

Coming
October 2000

Little Books for Busy Moms
Great Stories to Read and Fun
Things to Do with Them

Beth Lagerborg, General Editor;
written by Jane C. Jarrell

Reading opens the world to a child. Once you have the world opened, and you have piqued interest, how do you take the experience to the next level? Have you ever wished for something else to work with to further emphasize the lessons being taught throughout the pages?

Great Stories to Read and Fun Things to Do with Them makes a beautiful package by tying together children's literature with activities to reinforce the story. This book offers cooking, art, and moral principles as layers to build on after reading the suggested story along with Scripture from God's Word.

Softcover 0-310-23515-4

ZondervanPublishingHouse
Grand Rapids, Michigan

A Division of HarperCollinsPublishers

MOTHERS OF
PRESCHOOLERS

Little Books for Busy Moms
If You Ever Needed Friends, It's Now

Beth Lagerborg, General Editor;
written by Leslie Parrott

Written by relationship expert Leslie Parrott, *If You Ever Needed Friends, It's Now* meets the strong felt need of mothers of preschoolers to find and maintain friendships during this irreplaceable season of their lives.

Topics covered in this unique little book include:

- Motherhood: If You Ever Needed Friends, It's Now
- The Big Switch: Where Did All My Friends Go?
- 'Tis the Season: Friends of the Heart and Friends of the Road
- Kindred Spirits: Finding Friends Who Know "Mommy Speak"
- The Balancing Act: Being a Good Friend... and a Good Mom Too
- Wisdom of the Ages: Veteran Moms (Including Yours!)
- Friends in Low Places: Winning Grins Without Losing Your Friends
- The Homefront Friend: Befriending the Many in Your House

Softcover 0-310-23514-6

ZondervanPublishingHouse
Grand Rapids, Michigan

A Division of HarperCollinsPublishers

Little Books for Busy Moms
Kids' Stuff and What to Do with It

Beth Lagerborg, General Editor;
written by Leigh Rollar Mintz

All moms struggle to keep their children's possessions under control. They want to organize, but they are overwhelmed by the quantity of stuff that their children accumulate. *Kids' Stuff and What to Do with It* guides parents in this struggle to keep all their children's stuff organized. The book starts with creative tips on the initial approach to effective organizing and outlines basic organizational needs. *Kids' Stuff and What to Do with It* also gives great suggestions for organizing specific areas of the house, such as bedrooms, closets, and dressers or particular categories of items (toys, hobbies, and sports items). And finally to preserve the order that has been achieved, you are provided with helpful maintenance techniques.

Softcover 0-310-23511-1

ZondervanPublishingHouse
Grand Rapids, Michigan

A Division of HarperCollinsPublishers

This book includes a special "Mom's Moment" insight from MOPS, International

MOTHERS OF M♥PS® PRESCHOOLERS

Little Jesus, Little Me

Written by Doris Rikkers
Illustrated by Dorothy Stott

Smiling, laughing, learning to walk . . . Jesus once was a little child, too! With its simple words and colorful pictures, *Little Jesus, Little Me* helps your child relate to Jesus and sleep secure in God's love and in yours!

Board Book 0-310-23205-8

ZondervanPublishingHouse
Grand Rapids, Michigan

A Division of HarperCollinsPublishers

MOTHERS OF

M♥PS®

PRESCHOOLERS

This book includes a special "Mom's Moment" insight from MOPS, International

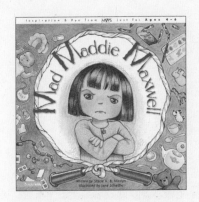

Mad Maddie Maxwell

Written by Stacie Maslyn
Illustrated by Jane Schettle

Maddie Joy Maxwell can't stop to talk and can't stop to play. Her jump rope is missing, and someone will pay! But who took it? Mom? Little brother? Big sister? Mad Maddie is about to learn that angrily accusing others isn't wise—especially when the real culprit's initials are M. M.!

Printed Caseside 0-310-23207-4

ZondervanPublishingHouse
Grand Rapids, Michigan

A Division of HarperCollins*Publishers*

This book includes a special "Mom's Moment" insight from MOPS, International

MOTHERS OF
MOPS®
PRESCHOOLERS

Mommy, May I Hug the Fishes?

Written by Crystal Bowman
Illustrated by Donna Christensen

While hugging the fish may not be one of them, your child is full of requests. And every yes or a no is an opportunity to learn about limits. Helping to bake a yummy cake is fun. But crossing the road without Mommy is dangerous.

Mommy, May I Hug the Fishes? is a colorful, creative way for your toddler to enjoy the fun of "yes" while learning that "no" has a reason.

Printed Caseside 0-310-23209-0

ZondervanPublishingHouse
Grand Rapids, Michigan

A Division of HarperCollinsPublishers

MOTHERS OF

M♥PS®

PRESCHOOLERS

This book includes a special "Mom's Moment" insight from MOPS, International

Inspiration & Fun from M♥PS just for **Ages 2 & Under**

My Busy, Busy Day

Zonderkids   Kelly A. Kim

My Busy, Busy Day

Written by Kelly Kim
Photographs by Bender & Bender Photography, Inc.

Dressing, playing, bathing, praying—every day is a busy day for your child! The colorful photographs and fun, simple rhymes in *My Busy, Busy Day* help your toddler connect pictures with words while celebrating the day's important activities.

Board Book 0-310-23206-6

ZondervanPublishingHouse
Grand Rapids, Michigan

A Division of HarperCollinsPublishers

This book includes a special "Mom's Moment" insight from MOPS, International

MOTHERS OF

PRESCHOOLERS

See the Country, See the City

Written by Crystal Bowman
Illustrated by Pam Thomson

The country and the city are very different, but both have colorful sights to see! In *the Country, See the City*, separate, imaginary walks through the country and town introdu your child to swishy fishes and cloppity horses, beeping cars and friendly policemen. T lilting rhymes and vivid, creative illustrations will captivate your two-to-four-year-old. A best of all, home is waiting at each journey's end!

Printed Caseside 0-310-23210-4

ZondervanPublishingHouse
Grand Rapids, Michigan

A Division of HarperCollinsPublishers

MOTHERS OF

M♥PS®

PRESCHOOLERS

This book
includes a special
"Mom's Moment"
insight from MOPS,
International

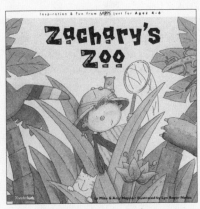

Zachary's Zoo

Written by Mike & Amy Nappa
Illustrated by Lyn Boyer-Nelles

Welcome to *Zachary's Zoo*, where a tiger, a bear, and a crocodile are among the ferocious beasts masquerading as lovable house pets. Only a smart, responsible zookeeper like Zachary can tame their savage nature by seeing that their needs are met. Letting the cat out, feeding the shark (oops, fish!) ... it's all part of taking care of the animals God made and gave to us as friends.

Printed Caseside 0-310-23208-1

ZondervanPublishingHouse
Grand Rapids, Michigan

A Division of HarperCollinsPublishers

We want to hear from you. Please send your comments about this
book to us in care of the address below. Thank you.

ZondervanPublishingHouse
Grand Rapids, Michigan 49530
http://www.zondervan.com